Evaluating Literacy

Evaluating Literacy
A Perspective for Change

Robert J. Anthony

Terry D. Johnson

Norma I. Mickelson

Alison Preece

University of Victoria
British Columbia

HEINEMANN
Portsmouth, NH

IRWIN PUBLISHING
Toronto, Canada

Heinemann Educational Books, Inc.
361 Hanover Street   Portsmouth, NH 03801-3959
Offices and agents throughout the world

Published simultaneously in Canada by
Irwin Publishing
1800 Steeles Avenue West   Concord, Ontario, Canada L4K 2P3

Figure 7–7 is reprinted by permission from Marty Woolings, "Writing Folders," *English Quarterly* 17 (Fall 1984).

Every effort has been made to contact the copyright holders for permission to reprint borrowed material where necessary. We regret any oversights that may have occurred and would be happy to rectify them in future printings of this work.

Library of Congress Cataloging-in-Publication Data

Evaluating literacy : a perspective for change / Robert J. Anthony . . .
  [et al.].
     p. cm.
   Includes bibliographical references (p.) and index.
   ISBN 0-435-08589-1
     1. Literacy—British Columbia—Evaluation.   2. Educational
evaluation—British Columbia.   I. Anthony, Robert J., 1946–
LC154.2.B8E93   1991
372.6—dc20   91-11368
                                                           CIP

Canadian Cataloguing in Publication Data

Main entry under title:

Evaluating literacy

Includes bibliographical references.
ISBN 0-7725-1900-5

1. Literacy—British Columbia—Evaluation.
2. Educational evaluation—British Columbia.
I. Anthony, Robert J., 1946–

LC154.2.B8E9 1991   372.6   C91-094859-3

ISBN 0-435-08589-1 (Heinemann)
ISBN 0-7725-1900-5 (Irwin)

Prepress work by Impressions, Inc.
Printed in the United States of America.
91 92 93 94 95 9 8 7 6 5 4 3 2 1

To the children and teachers in the schools of British Columbia, Canada, who, through their participation, contributed to a perspective for change in literacy assessment and evaluation.

Contents

Preface

*T*his is a book about the assessment and evaluation of literacy. It offers a perspective for change and challenges many current beliefs and practices. The aim is not to do old jobs better, but rather to look at assessment and evaluation from a new perspective. As knowledge about the nature of language and literacy acquisition changes, so, too, must assessment and evaluation practices.

For purposes of discussion, a distinction is made between *assessment* and *evaluation. Assessment* is used to denote the collection of information about children and educational programs, and *evaluation* to convey what is involved in the process of making judgments about that information. Although distinguishable in this manner, the processes themselves are closely integrated.

It is a basic precept of this book that educational aims or goals, curriculum implementation, and assessment and evaluation must be coherent. Educators, at whatever level of the system, cannot have one set of beliefs about the goals of education and the classroom practices necessary to achieve those goals, while at the same time assessing and evaluating progress from an entirely different perspective. What is offered in this book is not only a perspective for change, but also concrete suggestions for implementing that change in classrooms, schools, and educational systems.

Whatever our individual experiences with a place called school, to think seriously about education conjures up intriguing possibilities both for schooling and a way of life as yet scarcely tried. And, indeed, education is as yet something more envisioned than practiced (Goodlad 1984, 361).

So, too, with assessment and evaluation.

In Chapters One and Two, basic principles and current myths and misconceptions are outlined. A model of assessment and evaluation is developed in Chapter Three, and a data-gathering profile is outlined in Chapter Four. Chapter Five discusses the role of parents in assessment and evaluation, and Chapters Six, Seven, and Eight outline means of data collection and the interpretation of information gathered. In Chapter Nine, the integrated classroom is discussed, followed in Chapter Ten by a discussion of issues "that won't go away." In Chapter Eleven, responsive evaluation is highlighted. Finally, in Chapter Twelve, an action plan for change, both short- and long-term, is presented.

Acknowledgments

*M*any individuals contribute to the writing of a book. The children and teachers of British Columbia and colleagues in the United States and Australia cooperated generously in assisting us to formulate and implement many of the ideas and strategies outlined in this book. Professor J. Field, University of Calgary, Canada, participated in our early deliberations and was a rigorous critic for us. The following teachers are acknowledged with thanks: Principal Ray Rogers, Mary Tarasoff, and the teaching staff at Saanichton Elementary School, Saanichton, British Columbia; Dawn Jamieson, Armstrong, British Columbia; Yvette Gellatly, Richmond, British Columbia; Myrtle Miller, Vernon, British Columbia; Jane Chadwick, Diane Cowden, Myrna Jolly, Yves Parizeau, Linda Piccioto, and Margaret Reinhart, Victoria, British Columbia; and Andrea Lee, West Vancouver, British Columbia. We also thank Bronwyn Preece and Jennika Anthony-Shaw for permission to reproduce some of their work. Each member of our families was patient and understanding with our absences and preoccupations. Pat Chivers has earned our gratitude for her never-ending cheerfulness in typing this manuscript. To all of these, we owe a debt of thanks, and we acknowledge with gratitude their contributions.

Basic Principles

*T*his is a book about the assessment and evaluation of
literacy. It seeks to enhance and extend the best of current practice while
at the same time offering a perspective for change. The approach taken
is predicated on the belief that assessment and evaluation are integral,
planned parts of the curriculum and that children and their parents need
to be actively involved with the teacher in understanding, assessing, and
evaluating progress. Before considering assessment and evaluation, however, it is necessary to clarify the assumptions which underlie language
education and which must not be violated in any assessment or evaluation
program.

Language Education:
Underlying Assumptions

- The language arts (generally considered as listening, speaking, reading, writing and viewing) are interrelated. They are holistic in the
  sense that if they are broken down into bits and pieces, they no longer
  constitute real language. Separating language into its constituent
  parts, in fact, violates the integrity of language as language. It is rather

· · · · · · · · · ·
**Language
education is
holistic in nature.**

1

like breaking up a molecule of water (H_2O). If you separate a water molecule into its constituent parts, you no longer have water, you have hydrogen and oxygen. Or, if you take Beethoven's Ninth Symphony and break it into bar staffs, sharps, flats, chords or notes you no longer have a symphony. It is the way in which the components interrelate that gives the work its form. In other words, the whole is greater than the sum of its parts.

- **Literacy emerges.** Competence develops as an ongoing refinement process while children actively engage in language and literacy activities and interact with those around them in their attempts to understand their world.

- **Learning is a constructive process.** This includes listening, speaking, reading, writing, and viewing. The old notions of encoding and decoding have been superseded by the recognition that all learning is generative, or constructive, in nature.

- **Individual differences exist and must be recognized.** Emergent language and responses to literature are not standard—they are based largely on idiosyncratic, personal experience. This is not to say that there are not commonly accepted forms of language in the everyday world, or that hallmarks of growing maturity do not materialize as children become language users. But it is to say that children come to school with very different background experiences, and that the basis of excellent teaching is accepting these differences and building on them, rather than on denying them and trying to make them go away by forcing everyone into a standard pattern.

- **Language is the means by which children develop personal power in their lives.** Through their language, children give both form and substance to their thoughts, grow in their ability to interact effectively with others, and shape their personal realities.

- **Assessment and evaluation are not separate activities**—they are inseparable parts of the educational process. Their main purpose is to inform (in the broadest sense) educational practices and decisions.

Decisions about learning, teaching, assessment, and evaluation must be congruent. Therefore, when it is acknowledged that programs are holistic and child-centered, teaching, assessment, and evaluation must reflect holistic and child centered-perspectives. When pedagogical strategies underscore a belief that developing competence in all areas is an emerging process, evaluation must recognize this principle. Educators cannot espouse and implement one philosophy of learning and teaching, and evaluate from a totally different perspective.

Marginal notes:

· · · · · · · · · · ·
Literacy emerges.

· · · · · · · · · ·
Learning is an active, constructive process.

· · · · · · · · · ·
Every child is unique.

· · · · · · · · · ·
Language empowers children.

· · · · · · · · · ·
Curricular programs and assessment and evaluation practices must be coherent.

Assessment and Evaluation: Basic Principles

Assessment and evaluation are both process and product oriented. As teachers observe, collect information, and reflect upon, analyze, interpret, and utilize the information they have gathered in their work with children and parents, they provide demonstrations of growth and development.

Teachers are reflective practitioners.

Consulting with others can ensure that observations and conclusions are both valid and reliable. In so doing, educators are not preoccupied with statistical constructs, but with the more generic meanings of both *validity* and *reliability*. According to *Webster's New World Dictionary* (1964), *validity* means "well-grounded on principles or evidence; effective; cogent." *Reliability* means "that which can be relied upon; dependable, trustworthy." These are the characteristics which must define evaluation—like the programs themselves, evaluation must be well grounded on evidence that is both dependable and trustworthy. Someday, teachers and administrators will look back in disbelief at the faith they once placed in test scores and letter grades. The search for credibility in assessment and evaluation is pointing educators in a far different direction.

Validity and reliability are important.

There are certain basic principles which apply to effective assessment and evaluation programs in education.

Assessment and evaluation programs must be:

- centered in the classroom
- consistent with curricular goals
- consistent with what is known about human learning
- comprehensive and balanced

To accomplish these ends, all assessment and evaluation procedures need to be:

- numerous and multifaceted, leading to profiles of growth and achievement over time
- qualitative as well as quantitative
- reflective of the "constructive" nature of language
- collaborative (i.e., focused on the judgment of all those concerned—the learner, the teacher, and the parent)
- noncompetitive (i.e., focused on individual achievement rather than on comparative or competitive data)

- positive and helpful in leading to growth for the learner
- adaptive (i.e., shaped to fit particular circumstances)

Effective
assessment and
evaluation
programs are
planned.

Although effective assessment and evaluation programs are planned, there will be times when the unexpected occurs and opportunities arise for the teacher to evaluate the growth and development of children. Full advantage should be taken of these opportunities. For the reflective practitioner, effective assessment and evaluation are action-oriented, ongoing, and evolving.

The notion of teacher as researcher is currently in vogue. This book, however, embraces not only the teacher, but also the administrator, child, and parent. These stakeholders are not researchers in the traditional sense, but *searchers*. All have questions for which they need answers. In order to effectively answer their questions, information must be gathered, and evaluated and conclusions drawn. Everyone involved has a part to play.

Administrators

Administrators are
concerned with
systems analysis.

The question administrators ask is: "How successful is the program?" In seeking an answer, they need to undertake a systems analysis. As with all assessment and evaluation, the aims of the curricular program must be clearly articulated, information must be gathered on a systems-wide basis, and conclusions must be drawn about whether or not progress is being made toward goal achievement.

Teachers

Teachers focus on
individual children.

The teacher in the classroom is concerned with how well each student is doing and also, of course, how well the program is succeeding. In assessing progress, teachers must establish baseline data, gather information on each child's language repertoire, and finally evaluate to ascertain whether or not progress is being made. Specific techniques for teachers are outlined throughout this book.

Students

Self-evaluation is
important.

Self-evaluation is a vital part of any assessment and evaluation program. Thus throughout this book, strategies are presented which encourage

students to evaluate their own progress based on personal, ongoing profiles of growth and achievement.

Parents

In an effective assessment and evaluation program, parents are partners
with teachers. In fact, parents are a rich source of information and can
contribute much to the education of their children, to the evaluation
program, and thus, to the *searching* orientation involved in assessment
and evaluation.

Parents are partners.

Asking and answering questions is the cornerstone of effective educational assessment and evaluation.

In subsequent chapters, a model of assessment and evaluation; a data-
gathering framework for use by teachers, parents, and administrators;
and strategies for involving all the stakeholders are provided.

Chapter 2
Myths and Misconceptions

Shari was returning to teaching after seven years, during which time she had been busy as a homemaker and the mother of two children.

She was eagerly anticipating meeting her new colleagues and getting back into the swing of things, although she knew that a great many changes had taken place during her prolonged absence, and she was somewhat apprehensive about how up-to-date she was. Her principal had sent her an article, and she had felt a little confused about several statements:

- *the program is child-centered*
- *language is owned by the children*
- *language is a social phenomenon*

At the first staff meeting, a newly developed evaluation program was on the agenda. She particularly noted the comment, "This year in the primary grades, standardized tests will not be used." Shari's thoughts came in rapid succession. "Why aren't any standardized tests used?" "After all, wouldn't they be objective measures of achievement?" "Wouldn't the grade-equivalent scores be useful?" "How will I know at what level my class is working?" or "How shall

I group them?" "Oh, dear—things have changed so much!"
"Maybe I shouldn't have come back . . ."

. . . .

*D*ramatic changes have occurred in the teaching of language over the past several years as a result of emerging knowledge about how literacy is acquired. It is now known, for example, that in order to maximize achievement, children must be active in their own learning, must interact meaningfully with others in their environment, and must assume responsibility for their own actions and activities. No longer is the child fitted to a program—rather, the program is fitted to the child. In a very real sense, a successful literacy acquisition program is child-centered and holistic in nature. That is, it focuses on the child and is integrated across all curriculum areas.

In spite of this changing pattern of literacy learning and teaching, however, very little has changed by way of assessment and evaluation. If not the most critical issue today, this is certainly one of the most important. Even though teachers might embrace and implement holistic approaches to teaching, certain legitimate activities continue to be required of them. Children's progress must be documented, parents must be informed about their child's progress, and administrators must be assured of a program's effectiveness.

Teachers are accountable for what happens in their classrooms, and this is as it should be. A common way of considering evaluation is to suggest that it needs to be consistent with the goals of the program. In holistic programs, while consistency may be important, it is not an end in itself. As programs recognize the nature of language acquisition, an equally significant consideration is that literacy assessment and evaluation change accordingly. The characteristics that legitimize language programs, and that must provide an appropriate focus for assessment and evaluation, are the following:

- the program is child-centered
- language is owned by the children
- language in the classroom is meaningful and purposeful
- language is a social phenomenon

There are, however, several myths and misconceptions that have grown out of traditional assessment and evaluation practices. These need to be addressed.

Sidebar notes:

. . . .

Active learning requires active evaluation.

. . . .

Although teaching is changing, in many places evaluation is not.

. . . .

Evaluation must be consistent with what we know about learning.

Myth #1: **Assessment and evaluation are separate from instruction.**

It is common practice in many classrooms for the teacher to prepare lessons, teach them, and then test the children for knowledge acquired. This is done in a sequential, often hierarchical, way. Such procedures are unnecessarily limiting and fail to capitalize on the rich sources of information available in everyday classroom activities.

Assessment and evaluation in holistic programs, on the other hand, are part of the instructional process. They are ongoing and are centered both in the classroom and in the daily activities of the children. Procedures are qualitative as well as quantitative, multifaceted, and they focus both on process and product. In this sense, assessment and evaluation are not "snapshots" of achievement but rather are "videotapes" of performance. Thus, rather than attempting to record one moment in time, the teacher attempts to capture the child's shifting patterns of growth and development. As assessment and evaluation are ongoing, they form the basis of daily instructional decisions and unify curriculum and evaluation.

Education is not linear.

Myth #2: **Language is learned hierarchically; therefore, it should be tested sequentially.**

Research over the past two decades has shown conclusively that language is not learned in a linear fashion (Hall 1987). Language evolves as a function of meaningful, purposeful transactions between the child and significant adults, between child and child, or between child and print materials in the environment. Linguistic development is idiosyncratic and recursive in the sense that it emerges as a function of experience. To suggest that all children need to master the same skills in the same sequence flies in the face of current research. Yet many teachers and administrators persist in thinking that we can teach and test in this linear fashion. This leads to a third misconception.

Language is transactive.

Myth #3: **Tests tell us what children know.**

Of course, they do not. Tests tell us only what children know about a small sample out of a possible universe of discrete items chosen for the test, and only then if conditions under which the test is taken are optimal: if the child is not preoccupied with a personal agenda, if there are no health problems, or if the temperature in the room is appropriate, for example. Furthermore, in administering any test, teachers must be cognizant of such issues as the standard error of measurement and the suitability of the comparison of the class with the norming groups used in the standardization of the test. To suggest that tests tell us what children

"Tests tap too slender a slice." (Eisner 1983)

know, in fact, verges on the nonsensical! The Canadian Council of the Teachers of English (1985) policy on evaluation states this clearly:

> . . . The teacher's judgement must be the main determiner of the performance of his/her students, and he/she will employ a variety of measures and observations to inform that judgement. Tests or examinations extrinsic to the classroom should play only a subordinate role in any determination of student achievement.

Myth #4: **Evaluation is testing.**

Testing is only one small part of the process of assessment, that is, gathering information for purposes of evaluation. Testing, whether contextualized (developed in the classroom and based on classroom activities) or decontextualized (developed outside the classroom and not necessarily relevant to the curriculum being used) should *support* the teacher's judgment and never define it. The end in view is to develop a profile of achievement and to gather and record information that will demonstrate growth and identify those areas in need of attention.

Myth #5: **Standardized tests are objective measures of performance.**

Criticisms of standardized tests are legion, and it is increasingly evident that such criticisms are valid. Hoopfer and Hunsberger (1986) outline many critiques of standardized tests by numerous scholars, citing among other issues:

Objectivity is a myth.

> lack of objectivity, test bias, over-dependence on reading, over-dependence on statistical power, lack of breadth and depth of content covered, penalties for deep thinkers, penalties for careless bookkeeping, ambiguity of text and questions, reification of test scores, control of the curriculum by test constructors, lack of diagnostic value and information gain . . . decontextualization of the test situation, imposition of adult reality on child perception, limits to the certainty of assessment, incomplete use of rules during the testing and assumption that informational links are the same for all children.

Clearly, standardized tests are far from being objective measures of performance, in spite of the fact that they assume a mantle of precision that they do not possess and result in numerical scores. In fact, as the British Columbia Ministry of Education states:

> Anyone who works with measurements of any kind knows there is always a certain amount of error and inaccuracy associated with the

measurement process. This fact applies to measuring the acquisition of intellectual attainment in the same way it does to measuring anything else, except that an error in educational measurement may have extremely serious consequences for a child's future, in school and beyond.

Myth #6: Grade-equivalent scores tell us at what grade level a child should be reading.

This, perhaps, is one of the most serious misconceptions about evaluation because of the wide and erroneous use of grade-equivalent scores. Farr and Carey (1986, 153) deal at length with this issue, noting a statement by Walter MacGinitie:

> A student's G.E. is not an estimate of [his/her] instructional level. It is not intended to be. It is not a frustration level either. It is just a test score.

Farr and Carey go on to point out that the International Reading Association took note of the misuse of grade equivalents in a resolution adopted by the Delegates Assembly in 1981 (ibid., 154). The resolution states that "... one of the most serious misuses of tests is the reliance on a grade equivalent as an indicator of absolute performance." The resolution concludes:

Grade levels are administrative conveniences.

> Resolved that the International Reading Association strongly advocates that those who administer standardized reading tests abandon the practice of using grade equivalents to report performance of either individuals or groups of test takers...

Myth #7: Readability formulas are reliable and valid indicators of difficulty levels.

Such is not the case. Olson (1986, 8), in a study on readability formulas, concluded:

Who's to say what's difficult?

> The basic assumptions upon which readability formulas have been developed are indeed suspect and the conclusions and extended logic that have developed with respect to their current, and previous use are erroneous. The only reasonable conclusions that can be reached, based upon the findings, are that the readability formulas were based upon unsound criteria, that the correlation research to support the use of other formulas (strength by association) has similar weaknesses, and finally that the folklore extrapolated from the unfound assumptions places the questions of the use of readability formulas in great jeopardy.

And yet, educators continue to believe that they can assess with numerical precision the difficulty and suitability of reading material for individual children. In fact, only the students themselves can do so. Their purposes, background knowledge, and interests are important determinants in the selection of materials. Closely related to the notion of readability is grade equivalence, and this leads to a further misconception.

Myth #8: Tests determine appropriate grade levels for children.

This, of course, is nonsense. Grades are administrative conveniences. They simply provide educators with a way of handling large numbers of students. In our schools, of course, we have to group our pupils into "manageable chunks," and these are called grades. Substantively, however, a grade is what we say it is: no more, no less. There is no specific body of knowledge or set of skills that must be acquired during one specific year of a child's life unless someone says so. To look at a test score and assume that it tells us what should be going on with a group of children of similar age makes little sense. Rather, teachers should be guided by the daily behavior of their students as noted at home and school.

. . . .

There is no such thing as a homogeneous group of children.

Myth #9: Teacher observations are neither valid nor reliable.

It is only those working closely with children who can provide daily, ongoing information about student achievement and who can develop valid and reliable profiles of progress. It is commonly asserted that evaluation must be centered in the classroom. Using instruments that have been developed far from the classroom hardly satisfies this criterion. Rather, judgments about children must be made over time and should be based on a multiplicity of evidence. Smith (1986, 129) clearly asserts, "children do not learn better as a consequence of incessant testing." If evaluation does not benefit the learner, it cannot be defended.

Myth #10: Outsiders know better than teachers and parents about the progress of children.

If educators did not believe this, why would they so consistently depend upon tests developed far from the individual child, classroom, and school? Teachers and administrators who subscribe to this misconception will give undue weight to tests devised by people who know nothing of the local community; who have never met the children being tested; who know nothing of the students' backgrounds, hopes, and fears; and who are unaware of the aspirations that parents have for their children. Indeed, there is no "omniscient outsider" (Smith 1986, 125) who can do this job.

Assessment and evaluation must be child-centered, focused on the student in the classroom, result in descriptive profiles of achievement, and respect the professional judgment of teachers. If assessment and evaluation meet these criteria, they are far better handled than ever before and are consistent not only with the goals of holistic language arts programs, but also with an evolving philosophy of child-centered education.

Rigor is not abandoned.

Chapter 3

A Model of Assessment and Evaluation

· ·

Marie entered her new school with enthusiasm and high expectations for a great year. She and her husband had moved to Victoria from Vanderhoof, and she had been fortunate to secure a position in the district.

She met several of her new colleagues as she proceeded to the staff room for the first faculty meeting.

She looked at the agenda eagerly and felt somewhat dismayed to note that the first item was "Testing Program." Her heart sank as she read further:

September:	*Readiness testing*
October:	*Canadian Test of Basic Skills*
November:	*First report due by the 15th. Marks and grades due in the office by the 10th.*
December:	*Mid-year exams*
January:	*District Skills Test*
February:	*Second report due. Marks due in the office by February 9th.*

As the meeting began—and after greetings from the principal—Marie raised her hand timidly. "I teach kindergar-

ten," she said. "Does this program apply to me as well?" Marie's heart was beating rapidly as she waited expectantly for the answer.

. . . .

*I*n order to mount an effective evaluation program, it is necessary to conceptualize the entire educational process. This can be done by developing a model of evaluation which will enable teachers and administrators to implement an effective program.

Assessment and evaluation are integral parts of the curriculum. Essentially *evaluation* means "value from." In assessing student achievement or program performance, educators are attempting to ascertain whether or not value has been received from the educational experiences provided for children.

Evaluation in holistic programs must be data driven.

The model presented in the following pages provides a forum for discussion and planning by individual teachers and schools. It uses a common base of assumptions that every educational community must have in order to develop an effective evaluation program. A good deal of the underuse and misuse of assessment information is due to different members of the educational community holding unexamined, conflicting assumptions regarding the nature and purpose of evaluation.

Educators bring to their profession a set of beliefs which form the theoretical and philosophical foundations of everything they do in education. This is illustrated in Figure 3–1.

Evaluation is dynamic.

Theoretical and philosophical foundations do not stand alone, however. They are affected by social and political pressures, emerging research, and advances in theory. In Figure 3–2 (p. 18), these factors are represented by arrows that impinge upon and modify foundational beliefs. Information from all the sources is continuous and requires constant readjustment. Thus the model is not static but responds to changing conditions and influences. The model, in fact, resides not on paper but in the minds of members of the educational community, and is manifest in their actions.

If you don't know where you are going you'll never know if you've arrived.

Before any evaluation is undertaken, it is essential to be explicit about the overall aims of education. This leads to specific curricular goals, which in turn determine the materials and methods used to accomplish them.

Data must be collected on individual student performance and achievement in a way that addresses both process and product. Infor-

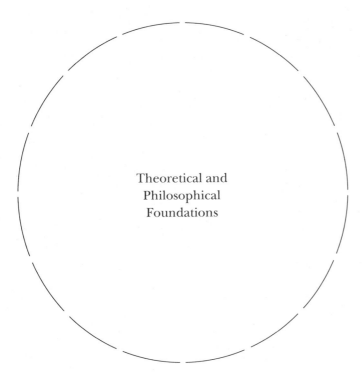

Theoretical and
Philosophical
Foundations

Figure 3-1 **Belief System**

mation should be gathered over time, so that it ultimately results in a profile of achievement.

Because profiles of achievement sometimes become voluminous, the samples of pupil activities must be selected and interpreted. Only then does the process of evaluation take place (Figure 3–3, p. 19).

Finally, after a pupil's achievement has been evaluated, accommodation may need to be made either to the curricular goals, the materials, or the methods used. If progress towards the overall aims is not evident from the assessment profile, then, clearly, changes need to be made. Only those closest to the learner—that is, the teacher in collaboration with the child and the parents, can make these determinations. No single test or measure can do so in and of itself. While tests may be used to support teacher observations, they cannot be used to define progress in absolute terms (Figure 3–4, p. 20).

The general model of assessment and evaluation that is depicted in Figure 3–5 (p. 21) schematically outlines these processes. Arrows symbolize the general sequence of events.

The implications of evaluation are not always comfortable.

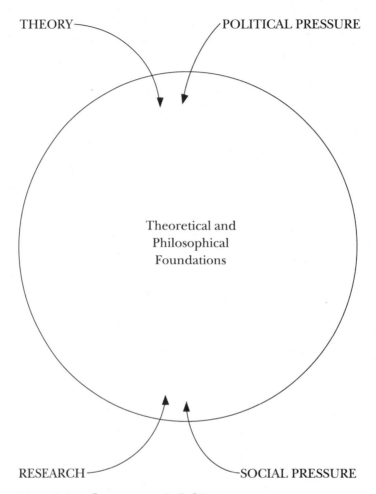

THEORY

POLITICAL PRESSURE

Theoretical and
Philosophical
Foundations

RESEARCH

SOCIAL PRESSURE

Figure 3–2 **Influences on a Belief System**

The model is regarded as a recursive, permeable loop that feeds on itself and is fed by information and influence from the wider society. These processes are meaningful only when they are coherent with all other aspects of education.

Negotiation, sharing, and reporting are included in the model. Negotiation occurs among constituent members of the educational community in establishing aims, determining curriculum goals, and deciding on forms of data gathering.

The sharing of information may occur at various points in the assessment and evaluation cycle. Normally, parents receive information after

· · · · · · · · · ·

The model represents an ecological view of assessment and evaluation.

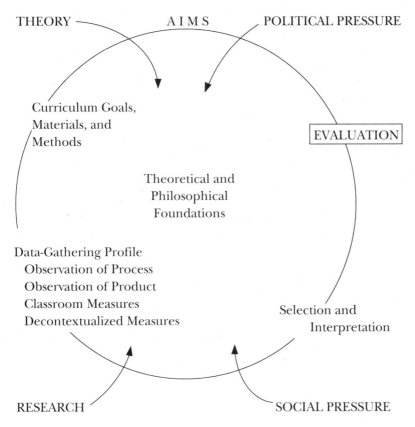

THEORY   A I M S   POLITICAL PRESSURE

Curriculum Goals,
Materials, and
Methods

EVALUATION

Theoretical and
Philosophical
Foundations

Data-Gathering Profile
    Observation of Process
    Observation of Product
    Classroom Measures
    Decontextualized Measures

Selection and
Interpretation

RESEARCH   SOCIAL PRESSURE

Figure 3–3 **Implementation**

it has been interpreted and evaluated. However, any parent has the right to see the raw data upon which interpretations and judgments are based. For example, if a parent questions a lack of growth in writing, the child's portfolio with samples of writing from throughout the reporting period should be made available.

A teacher may share information with a colleague or administrator in order to seek help in interpreting it. For example, a tape recording of oral reading might be full of dysfluencies. However, a colleague who has had experience with miscue analysis might notice that the majority of the miscues are meaningful and, in fact, are self-corrected. Thus while the child's performance might not seem impressive, there are clear indications that the student is in command of a number of self-generating reading strategies and that the prognosis for growth is good.

Accommodation involves all the changes that result from becoming

Receiving accurate information is a parental right, not a privilege.

Evaluation is interpretation.

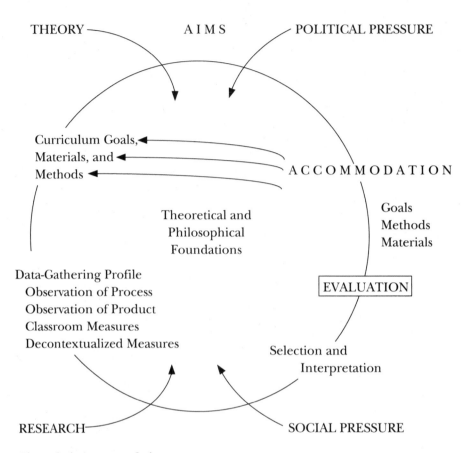

THEORY ── A I M S ─ POLITICAL PRESSURE

Curriculum Goals,
Materials, and
Methods ── A C C O M M O D A T I O N

Theoretical and
Philosophical
Foundations

Goals
Methods
Materials

EVALUATION

Data-Gathering Profile
  Observation of Process
  Observation of Product
  Classroom Measures
  Decontextualized Measures

Selection and
  Interpretation

RESEARCH ── SOCIAL PRESSURE

Figure 3-4 **Accommodation**

. . . .

**Action follows
from evaluation.**

aware of the implications of the evaluation process. In the unlikely event
that the evaluation indicates the program is working perfectly for the
child, the information is assimilated and the system is simply maintained.
However, if the evaluation process indicates both strengths and weaknesses, then appropriate action must be taken. Accommodation is a crucial
link in the evaluation/instructional cycle.

Notice that negotiating, sharing, and reporting are included in the
model. This simply means that all the stakeholders should be involved in
the evaluative process—children, teachers, parents, and administrators.

Putting a model of assessment and evaluation on a two-dimensional
page creates problems in terms of depicting the recursive and transac-
tional nature of the model. It should always be remembered that this
model of evaluation is dynamic. It changes constantly, depending upon

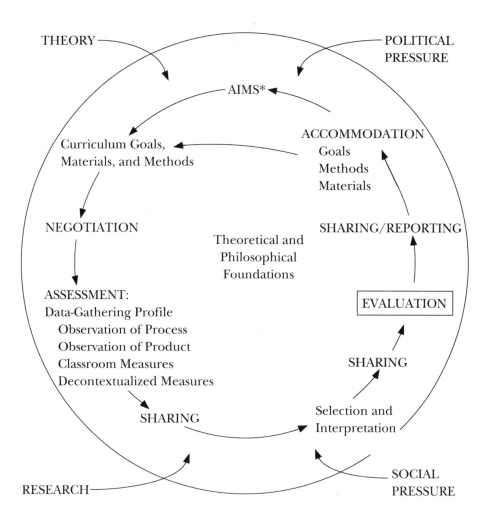

THEORY

POLITICAL PRESSURE

AIMS*

ACCOMMODATION
Goals
Methods
Materials

Curriculum Goals,
Materials, and Methods

NEGOTIATION

SHARING/REPORTING

Theoretical and
Philosophical
Foundations

ASSESSMENT:
Data-Gathering Profile
   Observation of Process
   Observation of Product
   Classroom Measures
   Decontextualized Measures

EVALUATION

SHARING

SHARING

Selection and
Interpretation

RESEARCH

SOCIAL
PRESSURE

*Begin with the overall aims

Figure 3–5 **Model of Assessment and Evaluation**

the context of the evaluation, its purposes, and the influences that are brought to bear on the teacher, the school, and the entire educational community.

Until assessment and evaluation are seen to be classroom, search-oriented, active processes of making judgments that involve all the participants, and that are integral parts of the curricular process, it is doubtful whether change can or will occur in our schools. Ultimately, what is taught in the classroom will be determined by the assessment and evaluation

· · · · · · · · · · ·
Evaluation controls curriculum.

programs used, and if changes are to be made in educational practices, evaluation procedures must also change.

Chapters Four through Nine carry a logo that represents the general model of evaluation (Figure 3–5). A shaded portion on the logo will symbolize which part of the model is being addressed in a given chapter. For example:

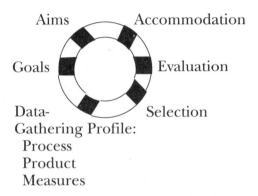

Aims　　　　　Accommodation

Goals　　　　　　Evaluation

Data-　　　　　Selection
Gathering Profile:
　Process
　Product
　Measures

The following narrative is based on a real-life case study. It is presented to demonstrate that while the model itself is an abstraction, it results in concrete decisions, actions, and consequences in the real world.

The fifth-grade teacher at Pentonville Elementary School had her students keep a log of home-based activities. When the class categorized and graphed the results, she was struck by the low level of voluntary reading reported. Reading was among the least favored recreational pastimes.

The classroom project is an example of *data gathering, interpretation,* and *evaluation.*

Sharing of data.

When she raised her findings and concern at a staff meeting, several other teachers expressed similar concerns. The principal noted that some parents were worried by several articles in the local newspaper on rising rates of illiteracy. The librarian, who was new to the school, said that he thought the number of books voluntarily checked out of the school library was at a lower level than at other schools in his experience. As

Implicit in the concern expressed by the teachers is the *aim of the school* that children should become educated adults. This broad aim is interpreted as a curricular goal that children would become habitual readers. Habitual reading means that children should sometimes choose reading as a recreational activity.

The media articles and the comments from the parents are an example of *political* and *social pressure.*

a result of this discussion, the staff decided to administer a survey of reading habits. The results confirmed the low level of home reading.

Data gathering and interpretation.

One of the primary teachers, who had recently attended a summer institute in language arts, reported to the staff that skill learning involved a much higher level of practice related to instruction, a ratio of approximately 80% practice to 20% instruction. Surveys of classrooms indicated that teachers use about 70% of the talk time. The children share the rest. If talk is equated with instruction, then the practice/instruction ratio is almost the reverse of what it ought to be. After some discussion, it was decided that the school could not provide sufficient practice time in reading. Clearly, something had to change. The principal reported on a parent involvement reading program in England that had been remarkably effective in raising the reading achievement level of the children involved.

Theory. This theoretical statement is based on a survey of several forms of skill learning.

Research. Goodlad (1984), Wells (1986), and many others document the predominance of teacher talk.

The staff recognizes the need for *accommodation.*

Research. The Dagenham project, Topping and Wolfenden (1985).

A school-wide parent involvement reading program was devised. Books were sent home to be shared, read by the child and/or by the parent. The parent signed a line on a sheet of paper whenever parent and child spent 15 to 20 minutes sharing a book together. A simple reward system was devised to encourage continued participation.

Accommodation. The school staff, having identified a problem and a possible solution, took action.

The program was implemented. Participation was voluntary. Some parents said that they were already reading on a regular basis with their children and didn't see the need for external rewards.

Negotiation. The stakeholders negotiated their level of involvement.

The program ran for a school year. Achievement testing showed a noticeable improvement in mean performance. A survey of parents suggested that those who participated, enjoyed it. The school librarian reported that the number of books checked out had increased by 35%.

Data gathering. Three types of data were collected.

A newsletter summarizing these findings was sent home. A copy of the newsletter was also sent to the school board office. The curriculum coordinator included a description of the project and its results in the district monthly bulletin.

Sharing. The results were communicated to parents and colleagues.

As a result, the school maintained the program as a regular feature of its offerings. Several other schools in the district developed modified versions of the program.

Accommodation. One school maintained a successful program. Others accommodated by emulating this successful practice.

Chapter *4* ....

Portfolio Assessment: Data Gathering— A Classroom Approach

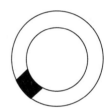

....

Bronwyn did not simply dislike report card time. She actually hated it. She knew very well that in her assessment and evaluation program, she should collect multiple sources of data from a variety of contexts over an extended period of time—and she had done so. For Jennika, the first child on her list, she had:

> *12 personal narratives*
> *1 report on "The Salmon" (47 pages)*
> *2 photographs of models of a fur-trading fort*
> *7 maps*
> *1 literary sociogram*
> *3 tape recordings of oral reading*
> *1 Informal Reading Inventory report*
> *9 spelling test scores*
> *2 unit test scores for social studies*
> *1 set of Canadian Test of Basic Skills scores*
> *1 tangram*

The file was about an inch thick. Bronwyn spread it out randomly on the table and despaired. What did it all mean?

What did this disjointed set of scores, records, and products add up to? How adequately did it reflect the bright little girl who came each day with a smile and a gossipy story about her family?

Bronwyn thought of the other 27 files, equally thick, waiting in the file drawer. She laid her head gently on her arms and sighed.

. . . .

*T*his chapter presents a framework for gathering and organizing information about student learning. The focus is on that part of the general model of evaluation called Data Gathering (Figure 3–5). The framework and the suggestions for implementing it represent for teachers a practical classroom-based approach that incorporates the principles of assessment and evaluation previously described. By using the framework in a classroom, the teacher is rewarded with a rich portfolio of information on student learning. The value of the framework can best be seen in relation to some basic questions that underlay its development: How much information is needed for evaluation? What sort of information needs to be included? Will the information be informative?

In presenting this framework, it has been recognized that teachers hold widely differing beliefs about what constitutes appropriate learning, teaching, assessment, and evaluation. Furthermore, it is clear that no teacher or theorist has discovered the ultimate solution to resolve the diversity of demands that characterize assessment and evaluation. Each member of the educational community tries to enact what are believed to be the best choices available. Therefore, the "best" scheme is one that allows every teacher to construct a personal best option. However, not all potential solutions are equally appropriate. The principles previously described differentiate those options that seem better than others. Even so, there are many other potential approaches that could be used. In the end, it must be recognized that it is natural for educators to hold differing beliefs about assessment and evaluation. The following scenario illustrates these perspectives.

Teachers hold a variety of views about learning.

Assessment involves choice.

A meeting of Josephine's third grade teacher, the fourth grade teacher, the principal, and Josephine's mother is planned. Each one has been asked to review a file of information in considering Josephine's future.

Third Grade Teacher Mary Simmons' Thoughts

Josephine's test scores are not very good, although she did quite well on the test I made up on *Storm Boy*. Her writing has really come along. She is using a much wider range of vocabulary than she did earlier in the year. She is learning to control plot and has branched out into expository writing in the last month. She's quite popular. I wonder if she would miss her friends if I held her back. Ethel does place a lot of emphasis on skills.

Fourth Grade Teacher Ethel White's Thoughts

Josephine's spelling is atrocious. If she comes into my room, she won't be able to keep up. Her handwriting is worse. I do wish other people would do their work. Her oral reading is surprisingly good considering the level of her written work. Her reading in June is really quite fluent. But then there are the test scores.

Principal Harry Underhill's Thoughts

Josephine's test scores put her in the second stanine. If she moves up, she'll pull the school's mean score down. However, if she goes into the 3–4 program, she won't be included in the district-wide survey. And the fourth grade teacher will have a large class. But will I get any static from her parents? Her grandfather is on the council.

Josephine's Mother's (Mrs. Bilker Peterout's) Thoughts

There's that costume we made. She worked hours on that. I've never seen her so keen. And then there are those stories. I didn't know she could write stories like that. They're really good. But then there are those reading scores. They seem so low. She seems to read all right at home. As I remember, she wrote those tests in February, when we were having all that trouble with her dad. Still, I suppose these teachers know what they're doing.

Josephine's Thoughts

Please, please don't let them put me in the dummy class. I'll just die. Janice will be smirking all over her silly face. What about Jean and Avril? I won't see them. What will happen to the reporter's club? Please, please . . .

Commentary

Each stakeholder approaches the same information differently. Each has valid concerns. All are selective in the weight they assign to a particular piece of evidence. Somehow, each individual must set aside a personal agenda and determine which decision is in Josephine's best interests. Each stakeholder, including Josephine, has a view that would enrich the views of the others if shared. The pooling of views will ensure that the full variety of information available is given due consideration in arriving at a decision.

When evaluating student performance, it is important to be mindful of the expectations of others. Education is a collaborative venture which includes many different partners. It is because each of the other stakeholders has a legitimate right to be well-informed about the progress of children that teachers should anticipate a variety of points of view when collecting information for evaluation. In order to meet these diverse demands, the bases of assessment and evaluation need to be broadly inclusive. Because of this, the evaluation framework that is presented here is intended to accommodate a broad range of perspectives.

Stakeholders collaborate in assessment.

Diversity of opinion is not the only reason to propose an inclusive approach to assessment and evaluation. Any single item of information about a student's learning is only a miniscule sample of that individual's accomplishments. The more information included, the more complete will be the picture of the student.

More is not necessarily better.

The goal of an inclusive approach to assessment and evaluation is gaining acceptance. However, the unbridled accumulation of assessment information could lead to an unmanageable jumble of demands, such as those depicted in Figure 4–1, and could result in the teacher becoming little more than an evaluation clerk.

There must be a counterbalance to unrestrained inclusion, and this is selection—a process that is required of every teacher. Through selection, the array of information gathering will differ in every classroom. In this way, both assessment and evaluation become individualized, with teachers exercising their professional judgment to develop a workable scheme in response to the needs of the school, the parents, and the students. No matter how carefully information is selected, however, results can at best give only a glimpse of the whole child. Evaluation is never complete.

Assessment is responsive to local needs.

Developing an assessment and evaluation scheme involves tension between inclusion and selection. It is this tension that can contribute to misunderstanding when stakeholders try to share information. That is, the information collected to meet the requirements of one of the stakeholders may not reflect the needs of others. This is precisely the reason that a systematic framework is needed: so that the different points of view can be accommodated in a coherent way. The following framework allows for inclusiveness, selection, and coherence.

Multiple points of view are necessary.

PERSONAL ANECDOTES   UNIT TEST   WRITING FOLDER   INTEREST INVENTORY   DIAGNOSTIC READING TEST   PARENT–TEACHER INTERVIEW NORM REFERENCED TEST   BASAL READER LEVELS TEST   PEER REPORTS   PERSONAL READING LIST   TEACHER'S MARK BOOK   STORY RETELLINGS   METROPOLITAN ACHIEVEMENT TEST   INFORMAL   READING   INVENTORY OBSERVATIONS   ON   THE   PLAYGROUND GRADE EQUIVALENT SCORE CLOZE TEST HANDWRITING SAMPLE   COOPERATIVENESS IN CLASS   WRITING SAMPLES   PLANNING WEBS READING LOG   READING CONFERENCE   AUDIO TAPE   READING   CHECKLIST   ATTENDANCE LIST   SOCIOGRAM   TEXT RECONSTRUCTION PERSONAL   JOURNAL   READING   MISCUE INVENTORY   OTHER TEACHERS' COMMENTS WORK HABITS   GATES MACGINITIE READING TEST   PERSONAL   JOURNAL   SPACHE DIAGNOSTIC   READING   SCALE   SELECTED ASSIGNED PROJECTS ATTITUDE TOWARD SCHOOL   SOCIABILITY   ORAL READING TAPE SAMPLES FROM NOTEBOOKS

Figure 4–1 Assessment Demands

The Quad: A Data-Gathering Framework

Diverse
information
requires
organization.

The data-gathering framework presented here consists of four categories of information: observation of process, observation of product, classroom measures, and decontextualized measures. Because there are four categories, it is referred to as the Quad. What is particularly important about the Quad is that it characterizes a wide range of assessment procedures. This is readily seen in Figure 4–2. The categories represent significant distinctions between types of data.

In the next section, assessment procedures of each type will be briefly described. This will serve to define the categories of data further, as well as to illustrate the way in which several familiar assessment practices are incorporated into the Quad.

Data-Gathering Categories

Observation of Process

Teachers can
observe learning as
it occurs.

Teachers are in a particularly privileged position to observe children in the process of learning. This is because children undertake so many of their learning activities in the presence of the teacher, and because teachers are uniquely trained to understand the behaviors that are observed.

Even though the gathering of observational data by the teacher is an important source of information on student learning, it should not interfere with the central role of teaching. The gathering of anecdotal comments must be compatible with, rather than disruptive of, good teaching. Teachers should take advantage of natural breaks in the flow of the day to record noteworthy incidents. It is even more important for teachers, at times, to build in observational periods during which they free themselves from active instruction and assistance and simply watch what is going on. For example, on occasion, when all the children are reading, writing, or working on research projects, teachers can circulate among the children. At such times, they should resist the temptation to be actively "instructing." This is most easily accommodated when classrooms are set up in a workshop model.

Observation
informs teaching.

In general, there are two principles which ought to be considered when collecting anecdotal comments. The first is that observations should take place in authentic situations—those that are part of normal instruction. For example, a child's capacity to work cooperatively may be noted as she or he works with a group on a task that requires collaboration.

Anecdotal comments from
classroom observation
and reflection

Reading logs
Learning logs
Selected pages from notebooks
  or journals
Audio tapes
Pupil self-assessments
Writing folders
Interest inventories

Interviews/conferences:
student, parents and
other professionals

Responses to reading:
retelling, text
reconstruction

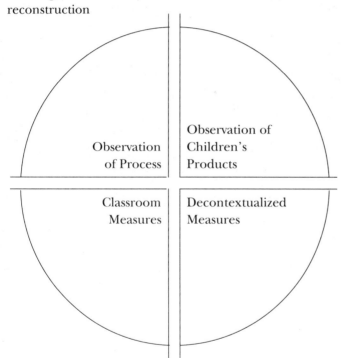

Observation
of Process

Observation of
Children's
Products

Classroom
Measures

Decontextualized
Measures

Text-related activities
Teacher-made unit
  (content-concept) tests

Criterion referenced measures
District or cross-grade
  examinations
Provincial or state examinations

Figure 4-2 **Data-Gathering Profile: The Quad**

Similarly, oral reading is best observed as it occurs functionally for children: when they are overheard reading, when they contribute information to a group, or when they participate in an oral reading activity such as readers' theater.

Patterns of
behavior reveal
learning strategies.

The second principle regarding anecdotal comments is that observations need to allow for making inferences about learning. The recording of anecdotal comments should be oriented toward interpretive questions, such as "Why did the student do that?" or "What general pattern of learning is exemplified?" Looking beyond the particular instance that was observed is important because in the end, it is the interpretation and explanation of patterns of learning that will establish the basis for evaluation and future instruction. It will not be possible to interpret every observation. Sometimes students do things which puzzle even the most experienced teachers.

Interviews and
conferences
provide unique
opportunities for
assessment.

There are many situations where observations of process can occur. For example, during interviews and conferences, a teacher might make observations about the child's enjoyment of literature, or about understanding of plot as revealed in the retelling of a story at a reading conference. The gathering of systematic, process observations is a rigorous task, but the richness of the information in guiding further instruction and evaluation is rewarding.

Observation of Children's Products

Products include such things as folios of writing, photographs of student projects, journals, taped samples of oral language, and plot profiles. These products should reflect a broad and varied sampling of activities.

Portfolio
assessment requires
broad sampling.

It is important to include information that is gathered by stakeholders other than the teacher. For example, the student could self-select work samples or a parent could contribute items. The inclusion of information selected by students and parents is an important feature of the framework. Any system of data-gathering that is consistent with the principles of evaluation referred to in the opening chapter must include opportunities for parents and students to contribute to the evaluation of achievement.

Classroom Measures

The most familiar examples of classroom measures are the various scores which are recorded for students on particular tasks. These scores can be obtained in several different ways. Among the most common are teacher-made tests.

Measures result in
scores.

Many forms of classroom measures are in common use. Scores are assigned to many forms of student work, such as projects and essays. The scores on exercises completed by students as part of their instruction are classroom measures as well. Later, in Chapter Five, several other classroom measurement techniques are discussed.

The fact that a record is preserved in the form of scores or letter grades reveals a basic contrast between information which is a measure and that which is an observation. The record of measures looks like a scorecard, while the record of observations looks more like a diary.

Decontextualized Measures

Decontextualized measures yield scores that do not originate in the instructional context of the classroom. The most common are state, provincial, or district tests. These are decontextualized because they are developed outside the classroom context in which they are used. Note that standardized achievement tests of various kinds are not included in the Decontextualized Measures quadrant simply because, as was noted in Chapter Two, they are not considered to be appropriate for assessing an individual child's progress. Standardized measures should be used for program evaluation or systems analysis. Their appropriate domain of application lies outside the scope of the Quad.

> "Omnipotent outsiders" (Smith 1986) do not know best.

Adjusting the Data-Gathering Framework to a Classroom

Although the framework shown in Figure 4–2 is symmetrical, it is applied in asymmetrical ways depending upon the age level of the students, the purpose of the assessment, and the context in which the evaluation is being conducted. In the primary years, for example, the emphasis might be on observation (Figure 4–3a, p. 34). In the intermediate grades, classroom measures might be added (Figure 4–3b). Gradually, decontextualized measures can be added with observational processes de-emphasized (Figure 4–3c) or emphasized (Figure 4–3d).

> Teachers emphasize that part of the Quad which is important to them.

The "balance" used is always dependent on the context in which the evaluation is being conducted and on the purpose for which it is being used.

> Symmetry is not the goal.

The identification of the particular weight to be applied to each of the four basic information types is only part of the selection process. In

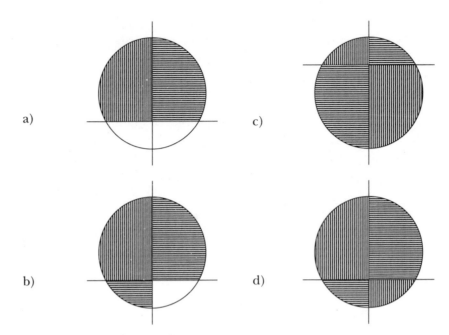

Figure 4-3 **Adjusting the Balance**

addition, each teacher is responsible for choosing data-gathering strategies within each of the four categories of the framework. One of the basic principles behind the design of this framework is to ensure that every teacher is free to exercise professional judgment in developing an array of information appropriate to the student. This process of selection ought to involve a degree of experimentation by the teacher familiar with data-gathering procedures. Attempts should also be made to search for alternative data-gathering techniques, some of which are discussed in Chapter Six.

When using this data-gathering framework, a considerable variety and volume of information can be collected. The most workable approach in managing this information is to have a folder for each student in the class. This is used as the central repository for the information, which will come from many sources.

Anecdotal comments recorded by the teacher are sorted and placed in each student's folder. Student logs, journals, and samples of work are collected from classroom work centers and stored, as are selected scores from the teacher's record book. As this information is gathered over the course of a term, the teacher monitors the relative frequency of each type

· · · · · · · · · ·

Judgment is required to achieve an appropriate weight.

· · · · · · · · · ·

Open a file on each child.

· · · · · · · · · ·

Variety is important.

of data and ensures that an appropriate variety is maintained. To check on this variety, a diagram consisting of four quadrants can be drawn on the outside of each student's folder, and as information of a particular type is added to the folder, a check mark can be placed in the appropriate quadrant (Figure 4–4).

By selecting an array of information over time, a profile of the pupil's achievement emerges. As the school year progresses, the content of the folder expands. Unless the information is periodically sorted, however, the mass of data becomes unwieldy. This review and sorting of information is conveniently done in conjunction with reporting periods or parent interviews. At such times, a few items of information from each category are retained, and the remainder of the information is redistributed or discarded. Over the course of a year and a succession of reviews of the student folder, a profile of the entire year's progress emerges. Such a profile can be passed on year by year as part of the ongoing evaluation of a student.

File contents are reviewed to keep the contents manageable.

This framework functions largely as a management scheme. Teachers should not become enslaved by the collection of information. Rather, the framework should allow teachers to collect data systematically. The improved variety and quality of information gathered will result in better,

The Quad helps the teacher organize the information.

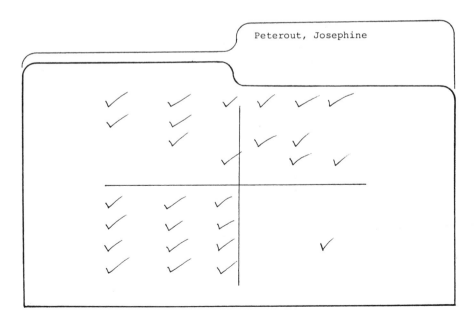

Figure 4-4 **Monitoring Portfolio Balance**

· · · · · · · · · · ·
**The Quad is easy
to use.**

more informed reporting and, in the long run, will save the teacher valuable time. The Quad can be used to organize data gathering in settings from early primary grades through university.

From this point on, the following logo will be used to indicate which part of the Quad is being discussed:

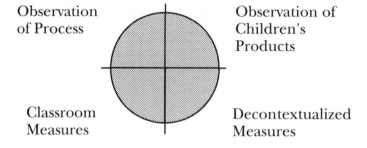

Observation
of Process

Observation of
Children's
Products

Classroom
Measures

Decontextualized
Measures

Chapter 5

Balancing Perspectives

They'd been right to make the change of schools, and this letter confirmed it for him. Mark read the form again. "What would you like us to know about your child so we can do a better job for him or her here at school? Please use the space below to provide any information you wish to share with us, and return. Many thanks." He couldn't help smiling, the contrast was so great. He couldn't imagine the teacher at Anna's last school sending out such a letter.

No, she figured her job was to tell parents what they needed to know. She did that, scrupulously, two times a year. Not that what she told them wasn't useful, but there never seemed to be an opening to mention Anna's worries about reading out loud, or her hatred of having her spelling score posted. He probably should have been more assertive: it wasn't fair to blame the teacher because he lacked the courage to bring it up. Still, this was a refreshing change, asking the parents what they want the teacher to know.

Anna was going to be all right in this new school. He had no doubts about it—not now.

*E*valuation should involve in a meaningful way those who are directly affected by the judgments made. When information, insights, and data are gathered from the key stakeholders, evaluation becomes more balanced, comprehensive, and trustworthy. At the classroom level, in addition to teachers, critical participants are students, peers, and parents. All offer differing perspectives, and all need to be acknowledged as potential sources for information.

All stakeholders
should be involved.

Naturally, different evaluative purposes require a different weighting of the information that is solicited from the various sources. For example, peer response is significant when a young writer wishes to determine the success of a story s/he has just read aloud to the class; it plays almost no role in determining whether a student utilizes a variety of strategies when attempting to comprehend what has been read. Similarly, if appropriate instructional decisions are to be made, there are many situations in which a learner's self-evaluation of performance and progress needs to be considered as carefully as the teacher's assessment. Furthermore, peers and parents frequently are in a position to provide the teacher with information not otherwise accessible. The task facing the teacher is to decide what information is needed, who best can provide it, and how it can be obtained efficiently.

The child is the
pivotal stakeholder.

All too often, the teacher's perspective is overly represented. Sometimes, in fact, it is the only view considered. Comprehensive evaluation requires the inclusion and consideration of many viewpoints. What is needed are concrete, manageable, and informing ways to include learners, peers, and parents in the evaluation process. In the following section, two such strategies are outlined. The first solicits information from parents, and the second involves parents and students in the ongoing monitoring of progress.

All relevant
viewpoints should
be considered.

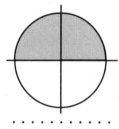

Parental Perspectives

Parents are
valuable
informants.

One of the easiest ways to gather information from parents about their children is simply to send a letter home asking for it. It is important that parents understand why they are being asked for information and receive an indication of the type of information desired. The tone of the letter is important; it should be inviting, sincere, and respectful. The letter should signal that the information provided will be valued, treated confidentially, and used to benefit the child. As sensitivity to the cultural and social backgrounds of the students is essential, letters and requests should be adapted in whatever ways are necessary to render them appropriate (see Figure 5–1).

Three points warrant comment. First, the two teachers who used this particular letter reported that almost all of the parents responded. While some sent it back with only a few brief remarks, others attached several pages of specific, detailed descriptions. Both teachers found that the responses provided them with background and insights that they could not have gained otherwise, and also that the letters gave them a head start on knowing the children.

· · · · · · · · · ·

Parents can provide information otherwise unavailable.

Second, this letter suggests possible topics, but the format is deliberately left open so that parents are free to decide what they wish to bring to the teacher's attention. Third, the letter offers parents ongoing participation and a meaningful role in supporting their children's learning

· · · · · · · · · ·

Invitations should be open-ended.

Dear Parents:

Children learn both at school and at home. Parents and teachers share the teaching responsibility.

Since we teachers contact students directly only during school hours, our reports are based on what we see during those hours. Children are at school for only six hours out of twenty-four for only 55% of the year!

We are interested in how you see your child at home. You might want to consider his or her social or academic development, interests, attitudes, strengths and weaknesses, and the like. Point form or brief comments would be fine.

Please bring your comments with you when you come to the report card conference, or send it in if you are unable to attend the conference. With your input we should then have a more comprehensive picture of your child as we discuss his or her progress and decide our joint plans for the future.

Child's name _____

Parent(s) responding _____

Date _____

Figure 5-1 **Inviting Information from Parents (Courtesy of Margaret Reinhard and Linda Piccioto, Southpark Community School, Victoria, British Columbia)**

at school. Parents are invited to bring the completed form to the parent-teacher conference so that their observations can be considered during the shared formulation of plans for the child.

Triangulated Observations

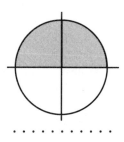

Collaboration is important.

The information-gathering procedure outlined in the following pages has been designed to systematically obtain, focus, and coordinate observations made by the teacher, the student, and the student's parents. The activity is meant to be a collaborative and mutually supportive endeavor.

Concrete examples are helpful.

Early in the first term, a letter such as the one in Figure 5-2, is sent home to the parents, explaining the project and inviting their participation. Included with the letter is a form that lists and briefly describes the behaviors parents are asked to monitor. (See Figure 5-3, p. 42, for an example appropriate for parents of children in the early primary years, and Figure 5-4, p. 43, for an example suitable in the intermediate years.) In constructing such a form, care should be taken to ensure that attention is directed to matters of significance, that the behaviors are concretely explained, that examples are provided where they are needed, and that educational jargon is avoided. In addition to being easily interpreted, the information sought should be manageable; nothing is gained if the parent is overwhelmed or intimidated.

Observations complement each other.

Over the designated period, the teacher also engages in systematic observation of the behaviors selected for monitoring. The teacher's findings for each student are recorded on a form similar to the one developed for the parents; however, the focus of the questions is more specific and sophisticated. (See Figures 5-5 and 5-6, pp. 44-45, for primary and intermediate examples of Teacher Observation Forms.)

The child, too, has a voice.

Next, students are asked to complete self-evaluation forms designed to probe their perceptions of their own achievements, attitudes, and interests related to the behaviors being monitored. (See Figures 5-7 and 5-8, pp. 46-47, for primary and intermediate examples of the forms.)

Communication is improved.

As confirmed by teachers who have used this procedure, its major value lies in the opportunity it affords for the sharing and comparing of perceptions. A regularly scheduled parent-teacher-child conference has proven to be an excellent forum for pooling and discussing the information obtained. Shortly before the conference date, therefore, it is recommended that the teacher send home a short note reminding the parents to bring the completed form to the interview (see Figure 5-9, p. 48, for an example of the note). An additional copy of the observation form

Dear Parents:

Your child will be involved in an exciting adventure this
year. S/he is continuing to learn to read, write, listen and
speak. While the prime responsibility for this important
learning rests with the child, you as parents and myself as
teacher will need to be aware, alert and supportive of the
learner.

Because we are all involved in this important learning
process, I have made observation guidelines for each of us.
We will all be asking how the learner is doing. We will all
be evaluating.

With this letter I have included my observational guidelines for parents. These guidelines focus on the types of
behaviours you may see your child involved in as s/he grows
and develops. You are uniquely able to see if your child is
using reading, writing, listening and speaking in everyday
situations - to see how s/he is really becoming literate.

Please refer to these guidelines when you are with your child
over the next three months. One week before the next reporting period, I will send another copy of the guidelines home.
Before you come in for our parent/teacher interview, please
take time to go through the guidelines and record your observations of your child.

At that time I will have completed a similar form and so will
your child. Consideration of the completed forms will contribute to our evaluation of your child's progress towards
literacy.

Yours sincerely,

Figure 5-2 **Letter to Parents, Early in First Term (Courtesy of Dawn Jamieson, Armstrong, British Columbia)**

should be attached in case the first one has been misplaced. By sending
the parent a second form, the teacher underscores the value placed on
the information requested, perhaps "reactivates" parental observation,
and saves embarrassment if the form has been lost or if parents have
neglected to fill it out.

The reminder letter also provides an opportunity for the teacher to
suggest that the child attend the reporting conference. Ideally, this conference should include the teacher, the parents, and the student, in order
to make possible a three-way exchange of information gathered. Such an

· · · · · · · · · · ·

**Aim for parent-
teacher-child
conferences.**

MY CHILD AS A LEARNER

Name _____   Date _____

Grade_____

Indicate your observation of your child's learning in the following areas. Please comment where appropriate.

	Yes/No	Comments/Examples
1. MY CHILD LIKES TO LISTEN TO ME READ TO HIM/HER.		
2. MY CHILD LIKES TO READ TO ME.		
3. MY CHILD TRIES TO READ IN EVERYDAY SITUATIONS (STREET SIGNS, CEREAL BOXES, STORE SIGNS).		
4. IT IS CLEAR FROM THE WAY MY CHILD TALKS THAT A BOOK HAS BEEN UNDERSTOOD.		
5. MY CHILD TRIES TO FIGURE OUT NEW WORDS FOR HIM/HERSELF WHEN READING.		
6. MY CHILD SOMETIMES GUESSES AT WORDS BUT THEY USUALLY MAKE SENSE.		
7. MY CHILD SOMETIMES CHOOSES TO WRITE.		
8. MY CHILD LIKES TO TALK ABOUT & SHARE WHAT WAS WRITTEN.		
9. MY CHILD VOLUNTARILY TRIES OUT NEW WORDS OR FORMS OF WRITING.		

QUESTIONS:

Figure 5-3 **Observation Guide for Parents (Primary)**

THE STUDENT AS A LEARNER

Name _____   Date _____

Grade_____

Indicate your observation of the child's learning in the
following areas. Please comment and provide examples where appropriate.

MY CHILD:	Yes/No	Comments/Examples

1. MAKES RESPONSIBLE CHOICES ABOUT:
- listening (radio, records,
  tapes, conversation)
- reading (fiction, poetry,
  non-fiction)
- viewing (television,
  illustrations, gallery art)		

2. VOLUNTARILY SHARES HIS/HER IDEAS BY: - drawing - writing - talking		
3. EXPRESSES IDEAS: - in an understandable way - in an appropriate way		
4. EXPRESSES OPINIONS ABOUT: - reading (books, newspapers, magazines) - television programs - ideas presented at school		
5. INDEPENDENTLY SEEKS INFORMATION		
6. PERSISTS IN TASKS		
7. VOLUNTARILY ENGAGES IN READING AND WRITING.		
8. APPEARS TO BE CONFIDENT ABOUT HIM/HERSELF AS A LEARNER		
9. EXHIBITS CURIOSITY		
10. IS WILLING TO TAKE APPROPRIATE CALCULATED RISKS WHEN READING AND WRITING.		
11. LEARNS FROM ERRORS		
12. LIKES TO WRITE ABOUT		
13. LIKES TO READ ABOUT		
14. LIKES TO WATCH		

Figure 5-4 **Observation Guide for Parents (Intermediate)**

THE CHILD AS A LEARNER

Name _____   Date _____

Grade_____

	Yes/No	Comments/Examples
1. THE CHILD SHOWS ENJOYMENT OF READING, WRITING AND LITERATURE BY: - listening to stories, texts, poems - voluntarily producing written language - choosing to read during spare time - reading favourite stories/ poems/selections to others - sharing his/her own writing with others - reading and responding to the work produced by classmates - voluntarily reworking or revising his/her drafts		
2. THE CHILD SHOWS DEVELOPING CONTROL OF LANGUAGE BY: - using it appropriately in a range of different situations - demonstrating increasing fluency - using an expanding vocabulary appropriately - asking questions, seeking clarification - retelling stories - summarizing information - producing an increasing variety of written forms (e.g. stories, poems, signs, directions, reports, journals, jokes) - showing increasing sensitivity to intended audience - demonstrating increasing ability to produce coherent, extended discourse (oral and written) - increasing his/her use of conventional spelling - efficiently using multiple cueing systems in reading and writing (semantic, syntactic, grapho-phonemic)		

This child's strengths as a learner are _____

_____

Areas in need of attention and extra support are _____

_____

Figure 5-5 **Observation Guide for Teachers (Primary)**

THE CHILD AS A LEARNER

Name _____   Date _____

Grade_____

		Yes/No	Comments/Examples
1.	VOLUNTARY SELECTS LANGUAGE ACTIVITIES DURING FREE-TIME.		
2.	READS AND WRITES IN A SUSTAINED MANNER.		
3.	CHOOSES AND FINISHES LITERATURE SELECTIONS.		
4.	LOCATES AND USES LIBRARY REFERENCE MATERIAL.		
5.	WILLING TO UNDERTAKE A VARIETY OF EXPRESSIVE FORMS.		
6.	TRIES TO INCLUDE ORIGINALITY WITH EXPRESSION.		
7.	SELF-MONITORS AND SELF-CORRECTS EXPRESSION.		
8.	EXHIBITS AN EXPANDING RANGE OF VOCABULARY.		
9.	WILLING TO SHARE IDEAS AND OPINIONS WITH THE TEACHER WITH THE CLASS		
10.	SEEKS AND RESPONDS TO CORRECTIVE FEEDBACK.		
11.	MAKES USE OF COMPREHENSION PROCESSES WHILE READING.		
12.	CONFIDENT AS A LEARNER.		

13. READING INTERESTS INCLUDE _____

14. WRITING INTERESTS INCLUDE _____

15. TYPES AND TOPICS OF MEDIA SHARED WITH ME AND/OR THE

CLASS INCLUDE _____

This student's strengths are _____

Areas for attention are _____

Figure 5-6 **Observation Guide for Teachers (Intermediate)**

MYSELF AS A LEARNER

Name _____   Date _____

Grade_____

Please draw a face to show how you feel about the following
sentences about writing.

If you feel this way <u>often</u> draw:

If you feel this way <u>sometimes</u> draw:

If you <u>seldom</u> feel this way draw:

If you <u>never</u> feel this way draw:

1. I LIKE TO FIND THINGS OUT FOR MYSELF. I AM CURIOUS.	
2. I LIKE TO READ (I READ A LOT ON MY OWN; I ENJOY LIBRARY BOOKS).	
3. I LIKE OTHER PEOPLE TO READ TO ME.	
4. I LIKE TO SHARE MY IDEAS BY: TALKING DRAWING WRITING	
5. WHEN I'M READING OR WRITING AND I DON'T KNOW A WORD I TRY TO FIGURE IT OUT MYSELF AND KEEP ON GOING.	
6. I KEEP WORKING AT THINGS EVEN WHEN THEY'RE HARD.	

COMMENTS

7.   I ESPECIALLY LIKE TO READ, WRITE AND LEARN ABOUT
_____

8.   I AM REALLY GOOD AT _____

9.   ONE THING I FIND DIFFICULT IS _____

Figure 5-7 **Observation Guide for Primary Students**

ME AS A LEARNER

Name _____   Date _____

Grade _____

	Yes/No	Comments/Examples
1. I TRY TO MAKE RESPONSIBLE CHOICES ABOUT: - listening (radio, records, tapes, conversations) - reading (fiction, poetry, non-fiction) - viewing (television, illustrations, gallery art)		
2. I LIKE TO SHARE MY IDEAS BY: - drawing - writing - talking - media (photography, movies, video, modelling)		
3. I TRY TO EXPRESS MY IDEAS SO THAT: - other people can understand them - other people find them socially acceptable		
4. I LIKE TO EXPRESS MY OPINIONS ABOUT: - my reading (books, newspapers, magazines) - television programs and videos - ideas presented at school		
5. I LIKE TO FIND THINGS OUT FOR MYSELF.		
6. I KEEP AT THINGS EVEN WHEN THEY ARE DIFFICULT.		
7. I TAKE ON RESPONSIBILITIES VOLUNTARILY.		
8. I AM CONFIDENT ABOUT MYSELF AS A LEARNER.		
9. I AM CURIOUS.		
10. I AM WILLING TO GUESS WHEN I'M NOT SURE.		
11. I LEARN FROM MY ERRORS.		

12. I LIKE TO WRITE ABOUT
    _____

13. I LIKE TO READ ABOUT
    _____

14. I LIKE TO VIEW
    _____

Figure 5-8 **Observation Guide for Young Learners (Intermediate)**

Dear Parents:

It is almost time for us to meet and discuss your child's progress since the beginning of term. I am sending you additional copies of the observation guidelines so that you can have time to consider and complete them before our interview.

Please bring them with you when you come for your parent/ teacher interview.

I would also like to have your child join us. S/he will be completing her/his observation forms during school time this week.

I look forward to our meeting. It will be interesting to evaluate together your child's progress.

Yours sincerely,

_____

Figure 5-9 **Letter to Parents as a Reminder, Sent Prior to First Reporting Period**

arrangement has obvious advantages and is strongly recommended. When the person who is the object of the meeting is not excluded, information is less likely to be lost or distorted in translation, and the learner can be involved in formulating any plans or program adjustments intended for his or her benefit. If, for any reason, it is not possible to have the child present, then it is especially important that the information provided by the student on the self-evaluation forms be shared during the conference. As is demonstrated by the sample in Figure 5–10, these self-assessments can be very revealing, even with young children. Whether the student is present or not, some of the conference time should be devoted to discussing the implications of the child's observations and how the parents and teacher can continue to support and extend the child's learning. The gathering of information is useless unless it results in decisions and plans intended to enhance learning and teaching.

The three forms designed for the parent, teacher, and student share a common focus and, also, their contents overlap. The difference lies in their level of specificity. Because all three observers are monitoring similar behaviors, although from different perspectives, the forms will likely reveal considerable agreement and consistency. Confidence can be placed in the accuracy and reliability of any observations or perceptions con-

· · · · · · · · · ·

**Children's views
are revealing.**

· · · · · · · · · ·

**Overlapping
sources of
information ensure
reliability.**

Name__Shawna_____
Date__March 1987_____
Grade__grade 2_____

ME AS A READER
(An Observational Guide for Young Readers).

Please make a face to show how you feel about the following sentences
about reading. If you feel this way _often_ make: (☺)

If you feel this way _sometimes_ make: (☺)

If you _seldom_ feel this way make: (☺)

If you _never_ feel this way make: (☹)

1. I LIKE TO READ. (i.e. reading is fun; I get books from the library)	(face)
2. I LIKE OTHER PEOPLE TO READ STORIES TO ME. (i.e. I take books home from school; I ask my parents to buy books and read to me)	(face)
3. I CAN READ BY MYSELF AND WHEN I HIT A HARD WORD I TRY TO FIGURE IT OUT BY SAYING THE SOUNDS TOGETHER.	(face)
4. WHEN I DON'T KNOW A WORD I SOMETIMES JUST GUESS AND PUT IN A WORD THAT SOUNDS ALL RIGHT AND MAKES SENSE.	(face)
5. WHEN I COME TO A PERIOD I KNOW WHAT TO DO. (i.e. stop, take a breath, make my voice go down)	(face)

COMMENTS:

The best thing about reading is... 1 you learn new words evry day

The worst thing about reading is. 2 wen you find a word you don't no and and you guss and it dosint sontd rite it gets boring

Figure 5–10 **An Example of a Child's Self-Evaluation (Courtesy of Dawn Jamieson, Armstrong, British Columbia)**

firmed in this way (see Figure 5–11, p. 50). When the observations reveal discrepancies, the need for additional information and for further monitoring is clearly signalled.

The observational guidelines can inform parents indirectly as to which behaviors have significance for learning and school success. It is important that parents' attention be directed to things that matter and that the items

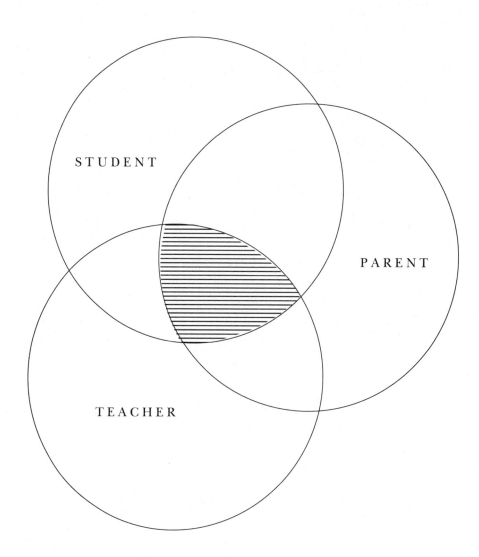

CONVERGENCE: CONSISTENCY: RELIABILITY

Figure 5–11 **Triangulating Perspectives**

. . . .

**Focus on what
matters.**

listed on the form reflect the approach and emphases of the classroom program. With this in mind, note Figure 5–12.

The first two behaviors listed reflect attitude: Does the child like to read and be read to? Next, the parent is asked to notice whether the child attempts independent application of his/her knowledge of reading: Does the child try to read the environmental print encountered? The funda-

MY CHILD AS A LEARNER

Name _____   Date _____

Grade_____

Indicate your observation of your child's learning in the
following areas. Please comment where appropriate.

	Yes/No	Comments/Examples
1. MY CHILD LIKES TO LISTEN TO ME READ TO HIM/HER.		
2. MY CHILD LIKES TO READ TO ME.		
3. MY CHILD TRIES TO READ IN EVERYDAY SITUATIONS (STREET SIGNS, CEREAL BOXES, STORE SIGNS).		
4. IT IS CLEAR FROM THE WAY MY CHILD TALKS THAT A BOOK HAS BEEN UNDERSTOOD.		
5. MY CHILD TRIES TO FIGURE OUT NEW WORDS FOR HIM/HERSELF WHEN READING.		
6. MY CHILD SOMETIMES GUESSES AT WORDS BUT THEY USUALLY MAKE SENSE.		
7. MY CHILD SOMETIMES CHOOSES TO WRITE.		
8. MY CHILD LIKES TO TALK ABOUT & SHARE WHAT WAS WRITTEN.		
9. MY CHILD VOLUNTARILY TRIES OUT NEW WORDS OR FORMS OF WRITING.		

Annotations to the right of the table:
- ATTITUDE (items 1–2)
- INDEPENDENT APPLICATION (item 3)
- FOCUS ON COMPREHENSION (item 4)
- STRATEGY (item 5)
- RISK-TAKING (item 6)
- SELF-INITIATED ACTIVITY (items 7–9)

QUESTIONS:

Figure 5–12 **Observation Guide for Parents (Primary) Signifying Important Learning Behaviors**

mental role of comprehension in reading is underscored by having the
parent consider how much understanding is demonstrated by the way the
child talks about the books encountered. This point is perhaps better
made by noting what is not stressed. For instance the parents are not
asked to record the child's knowledge of alphabet letters or the number
of sight words read off flashcards; rather they are asked to judge whether
the child responds meaningfully to books. The fifth, sixth, and ninth items
on the form are designed to focus attention on the strategies the child
uses: Does the child try to independently figure out new words when
reading and writing? Are context clues used? Risk-taking also underlies

items six and nine: Is the child willing and sufficiently confident to risk a logical guess when unsure or to experiment with new types of writing? The last items listed seek information about whether or not, and how, the child chooses to engage in writing at home. Attention is therefore drawn to self-initiated activities, and these obviously also reflect the attitude of the learner. The point is that parents should be asked to monitor those behaviors, attitudes, and dispositions that have long-term consequences for learning, that are valued by the school, and that they are in a unique position to observe. When devised with this goal in mind, the forms execute a double function: in addition to being information-gathering tools, they also can serve to inform and educate the parents who use them.

The guides elicit information and educate parents.

This procedure of triangulating observations—of gathering information from the parent, child, and teacher—has much to recommend it. It exemplifies the principle that evaluation should be based on the informed judgement of those closest to the learner. The parents are involved, informed, and included. The child is consulted and invited to reflect on and assess his/her learning. By having the parents, teacher, and child monitor selected behaviors over a period of time, one-shot snap judgements are unlikely. The focus is upon the learner's performance in the context of the real-life, everyday events that occur at home and in school. The information obtained is both valid and reliable, and far more trustworthy than that which results from tests taken under tense and unfamiliar examination conditions. The procedure supplies its own checks and balances and offers the richness and reassurance of multiple viewpoints. It also serves to open lines of communication: One of the main purposes in gathering the information is to share and compare. When parents arrive for the evaluation conference, they come prepared and are in a position to offer information rather than merely to receive it. The teacher is relieved of the burden of having to evaluate alone. Two of the most important features of this procedure are flexibility and adaptability. The forms presented are intended as examples only; they easily can be modified and reworked to make them fit almost any content area, grade level, or teaching situation.

Evaluation involves those closest to the learner.

The teacher should not be the sole evaluator.

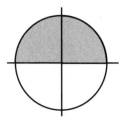

The Child as Evaluator

Young children are natural evaluators. Unfortunately, this is often unrecognized and sometimes discouraged at school. If our goal ultimately is to help develop students who are able to think critically, make reasoned, valid, supportable judgments; and be clear about the criteria upon which their judgments are made, then students should be provided with ample experience as evaluators. Students need to be given frequent opportunities to monitor, reflect upon, and evaluate their own progress, learning strategies, work habits, products, and achievements. Self-evaluation should become a key activity in every classroom. Students should be invited to evaluate the instructional materials with which they work and the learning activities they engage in and are exposed to at school. Several strategies and suggestions for facilitating evaluation by students are described in the following section.

Students should be given the opportunity to be evaluators.

Learning Logs

Learning logs are notebooks in which students periodically record their insights, observations, or feelings about themselves as learners and about what they are learning. Learning logs are intended to encourage self-monitoring and reflection. The teacher might, for example, begin by simply asking the students, at the end of a unit or an activity, to reflect on three things they have learned, or one thing they found confusing. If appropriate, the students may then be invited to compare their conclusions with a partner. With young children, the process can be conducted orally; older students may prefer to occasionally write their reflections and responses in a booklet specifically designed for the purpose. The decision to share the contents with other students should be left entirely to each student.

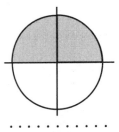

Learning logs inform both the reader and the writer.

A variety of different prompts or lead-in phrases can be suggested. By selecting the prompts carefully, teachers can encourage students to become constructively analytical about, and more aware of, their own learning styles, approaches, strengths, preferences, and shortcomings. For example:

Reflection leads to insight.

Preferences
The most interesting thing about was . . .
My favorite part of the school day is when . . .
My favorite kind of question is the type that . . .
I prefer to work by myself on activities that . . .

Learning Style and Strategies
When I have to do a project, the first thing I like to do is . . .
If I can, I try to avoid activities that . . .

I work best when . . .
When I don't understand something, I . . .

Strengths

I'm getting much better at . . .
One good question I asked (or thought of) today was . . .
One of the things I do best is . . .
I can help people in my class with . . .
I'm proud of the way I . . .

Areas in Need of Improvement

I need to work harder on . . .
I'm still not sure how to . . .
I need to get help with . . .
I wish I were better at . . .
The part I found the most difficult was . . .

Students should be invited to contribute interesting lead-ins of their own. As with anything, the procedure needs to be used sparingly so that it does not become tedious or degenerate into "reflection-on-demand."

The following comments, excerpted from the learning logs of junior high school students (courtesy of Julie Davis, Claremont Secondary School, Saanich, British Columbia), show how reflective and insightful students can be. The question posed was, "What is your favorite kind of question?"

· · · · · · · · · ·
Given the opportunity, students reveal their insights.

My favorite type of questions are questions that say What do you think? I like questions like that because they let me give my opinion with my own set of facts to support it. I also like them because I can go into more detail with the answers where if it was like What did so and so think? you're really not that person and you really don't know. I think opinion questions give me time to tell what I think on the subject and there's no right or wrong answer.

I like a question that is slightly cryptic and makes you think. Another question I like is one where there is no correct answer. . . . Puzzles have always appealed to me for the simple reason that you know there must be an obvious answer, through it may be hidden.

My favorite kind of question is one that I have to think about but not in great depth. If possible, I like to add imagination although I don't always use it.

My favorite kind of question is a question I know the answer to.

Learning logs can also be used to facilitate personal goal setting if a section of the log is set aside for recording goals and challenges. For example, one student might decide to improve the organization of an expository report, while another might set a goal of working cooperatively with a project group. Each student would then record relevant observations, efforts, and successes as they occur. Such logs can help students develop their sense of personal control over learning and provide them with a tangible record of progress toward something they have decided matters to them. Goodlad (1984) stresses the importance of involving students in setting their own goals and notes how rarely this was observed in his study of one thousand American classrooms.

Personal goals engender commitment.

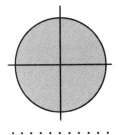

Discrepancy Checks

Report cards also can offer a very effective opportunity for student self-evaluation: students can be invited to write report cards on themselves. Although there are many ways that this may be handled, the following procedure is recommended.

Self-reporting promotes reflection.

Approximately one week prior to the sending home of the teacher-written report cards, students are given a blank photocopy of the report-card form used in their school. They are then asked to complete the form as honestly and thoughtfully as they are able, giving themselves whatever marks, grades, or ratings they feel their performance during the evaluation period warrants. They also are asked to write several comments. Two of the comments should note areas where the student feels s/he has done well, has made gains, or merits acknowledgment for effort or attitude; one should focus on an area where the student is experiencing difficulty or recognizes that improvement or additional effort is required. (See Figure 5–13, p. 56, for an example written by a student in fourth grade.) The procedure works best if the forms are filled in at home and returned the following day. If undertaken at school, it is important that the process be an individual activity with student privacy protected.

Completing the report cards can be a valuable self-assessment exercise. The procedure also affords the opportunity for the teacher to conduct a discrepancy check. Once the completed forms have been returned, the evaluations the students have given themselves can be compared with those proposed by the teacher. It is interesting to note that teachers report a high degree of agreement. The point of the discrepancy check, however, is to identify any students who have consistently rated themselves either more positively or more negatively than has the teacher. Mismatches may then be discussed on an individual basis with the students before the

Discrepancies require discussion.

School: Willows
Name: Bronwyn Preece
Grade: 4
Teacher: Yves Parizeau

INTERMEDIATE
PROGRESS
REPORT

EXPLANATION OF SYMBOLS
Individual Achievement
Teacher's assessment of
student's progress.

 A — Excellent progress
 B — Very Good progress
 C+ —
 C — Average progress
 C- —
 D — Below Average progress
 E — Unsatisfactory progress

Individual Effort
The teacher's assessment
of the effort the student
applies to the learning
process.

 G — Good
 S — Satisfactory
 N — Needs improvement

Greater
VICTORIA
School District

Authorized by the Board of School Trustees
School District No. 61 (Greater Victoria)

	First Report		Second Report		Third Report		Final Grade
	Individual Achievement	Individual Effort	Individual Achievement	Individual Effort	Individual Achievement	Individual Effort	
READING	B	G					
LISTENING	A	G					
SPEAKING	A	G					
WRITING SKILLS	A	G					
SPELLING	A	G					
MATHEMATICS	A	G					
SCIENCE	A	G					
SOCIAL STUDIES	A	G					
PHYSICAL EDUCATION	B	C					
ART		S					
MUSIC	C	G					
OTHER English	B	G					
WORK HABITS		G					
SOCIAL/PERSONAL DEVELOPMENT		G					

Comments

Unless specified in the teacher's written comments, the grades appearing in the
Individual Achievement and Final Grade columns reflect student mastery of Prescribed
Curriculum for the grade level.

Bronwyn likes to participate in
group activities with other
people.

    She also is at the satisfac-
tory level of art. Her pictures
have alot of time to them but
are not that good.

Figure 5-13 **A Report Card on Yourself: Fourth Year**

official report cards are finalized and shared. In some instances, it is possible that the teacher may have overlooked aspects of performance which deserve more credit than was granted. The student can thus be given an opportunity to attempt to justify his or her rating, and perhaps supply additional evidence. By the same token, if a student is expecting a better report than the one s/he is to receive, the teacher has the chance to become aware of this and explain why the evaluation is less favorable than anticipated. Such discussions with the teacher can clarify the reasons for the judgments made and help demystify what may well appear to some students to be a somewhat arbitrary process. Perhaps just as importantly, the discussions also can help the students explain their report cards to their parents.

Negotiation is possible.

Student-written report cards have been successfully used with students from first grade on. The report forms can easily be simplified to make them appropriate for use with young children (see Figure 5–14, p. 58) and teachers or assistants can act as scribes for those yet unable to write for themselves. Furthermore, these reports have been found to be effective and revealing when used with students of widely differing abilities. While Figure 5–13 presents a report written by a confident and successful student, the comments in Figure 5–15 (p. 59) were written by a student in the fifth grade for whom school represents a struggle. Students, regardless of ability or achievement, appear to appreciate the opportunity that writing report cards on themselves gives them to express their own opinions and perceptions of how they are doing in school.

All students can participate.

Preference Checks

Students should be invited to evaluate the activities and materials that are part of their day-to-day classroom experience. A simple way to facilitate this is to list a number of different activities (or centers or books) and have the children vote for their favorite or for the one they find the most interesting, useful, or challenging. Results can then be tallied, graphed, and displayed. Students can contribute to a class graph or survey (Figure 5–16, p. 60), or they can construct a personal one (Figure 5–17, p. 61).

The nature of the question posed will vary depending on the age and sophistication of the student and the nature of the information desired. For example, kindergarten children, given the choice of the block corner, the art activities, the water table, the woodworking bench, or the book nook, could be asked to choose the one center that they most enjoy. Older students could be asked to rank four different nonfiction books on animals according to the power and quality of their illustrations. Upon completion

Student preferences vary.

Report Card for _____

G = good
S = satisfactory, okay
N = needs to improve

Reading _G_   Behaviour _N_

Spelling _G_   P.E. _G_

Printing _G_   Science _G_

Listening _S_   Social Studies _G_

Speaking _G_   Art _G_

Thinking _G_   Music _G_

I like to _Play_ _____

I am good at _Printing_ _____

I have improved in _Spinning hoop_ _____

I need to _lisin_ _____

I could try harder to _work_ _____

Figure 5-14 **A Report Card on Yourself: First Year (Courtesy of Mrs. Myrtle Miller, Lavington Elementary School, Vernon, British Columbia)**

Comments

GRADE 5

Unless specified in the teacher's written comments, the grades appearing in the
Individual Achievement and Final Grade columns reflect student mastery of Prescribed
Curriculum for the grade level.

[handwritten student comment]

Comments

GRADE 5

Unless specified in the teacher's written comments, the grades appearing in the
Individual Achievement and Final Grade columns reflect student mastery of Prescribed
Curriculum for the grade level.

[handwritten teacher comment]

Figure 5–15 **A Report Card on Yourself: Students in Difficulty (Courtesy of Jane
Chadwick, Monterey Elementary, Victoria, British Columbia)**

In our opinion ...	the most INTERESTING ACTIVITY was:	the most CHALLENGING ACTIVITY was:
Interviewing the builders	● ● ● ● ●	●
Making a 'blueprint'	● ●	● ● ● ● ● ● ● ●
Building the model	● ● ● ● ● ● ● ● ●	● ● ● ● ●
Drawing the map	● ● ●	● ● ●
Measuring and staking the site	● ● ● ●	● ● ●
Presenting the model	● ●	● ● ● ●

Most people thought building the model was the most interesting activity and making the 'blueprint' the most challenging.

Figure 5–16 **Student Feedback: Class Record**

Mrs. Jolly
Clovdale School

Math	Sf	Math needs to be harder.
Spelling	VG	Spelling is fine.
Reading	VG	reading is good.
Maners	VG	Maners are very Good
Art	Sf	Art need more neet thing.

Figure 5–17 **Student Feedback: School Subjects (Courtesy of Myrna Jolly, Clo-verdale Elementary School, Victoria, British Columbia)**

of a thematic unit, students could rate the various activities to determine which the majority found most interesting (see Figure 5–16 for an example from a first-grade class). Where appropriate, students should be encouraged to explain the reasons for their choices.

The information gained from these opinion polls is often surprising. Many teachers have found that the results differ from their predictions. When thoughtfully drafted, preference checks can provide teachers with a great deal of information about student response and reactions to the instructional program. Such information is invaluable and should be noted by the teacher.

As is well-illustrated by the excerpt in Figure 5–18 (p. 62) from an interview with two nine-year-olds, children are capable of perceptive and insightful observations and evaluations of their school experiences. These students from two different fourth-grade classrooms were asked to describe the things they liked about school. Having done so, the topic shifted to some of the things that were not liked.

B. P.: And what I also don't like about it is that we don't . . all we do every time is we, when we get him, is we do the <u>speller</u>. We get our test, we do the workbook, we get our test, we do the workbook . . . . We don't do any creative writing with him or <u>anything</u> . . . nothing . . . . .Well, when I had a different teacher, um, we didn't have any spellers or a speller at all and we did a lot of creative writing and we did do some work though and then it was much funner and we actually did learn a lot lot more by creative writing . . . . I've found out, as I've done things by now going to the, doing speller instead of all this creative writing and things, that um . . . creative writing is a lot better to <u>learn</u> things with . . . . .

Adult: Why?

B. P.: Than, um . . . well like you have the <u>words</u> there that you're using and then like if you're spelling "saving," maybe, where it's something you have to add "ing" to, but you have to drop the "e" and you put, maybe, s-a-v-<u>e</u>-i-n-g, like the teacher can help you with correcting the words and then maybe you can see that <u>you</u> did that mistake and then you can also see the other words.

Adult: So you . . . are you . . . I'm trying to understand . . . do you mean it's easier to learn to spell when you're trying to actually write a story?

B. P.: Yeah. And the <u>speller</u>, I found out, it really doesn' help you that much.

Adult: Why? . . . Why? Why is that?

B. P.: Well . .. it . . . I have . . . like you're not <u>spelling</u> any bit . . . you're just completing things, like "Get the . ... Find the list word that means a baby horse." Maybe "colt;" or it may say "Three places that you can sleep for the night that is in your list words" and there could be . . . and what it may be is "tent," "cabin" and "cave" but like, you don't find too many people in <u>caves</u> or anything and . . . . It's really just completing assignments . . . you're not <u>learning</u> that much, anything, really . . .

Adult: Well, don't you think your teacher thinks you're learning about the meaning of those words?

B. P.: Well I don't think so, and I'm not learning anything.

Adult: Oh.

B. P.: Not anything.

Adult: Heather, do you . . . do you agree with any of this? Do you have the same sorts of feelings?

Heather: Yep. Our teacher does the same thing. All we do is . . like . . . like she says . . we have the questions and we just have to look for the list word and put it in . . . .

Figure 5–18 **Student Feedback: Program Evaluation (Recorded by Alison Preece)**

Teachers need to provide deliberately and regularly scheduled opportunities for students to formulate and express their evaluations of the learning experiences and materials to which they are exposed.

A Report Card on the Teacher

In many classrooms, it is the teacher who has the sole right to evaluate and report on others. The only role permitted students is that of passive recipients of teacher evaluation. One way to help students experience the complexities inherent in the process of judging another's performance and then sharing that judgment is for the teacher to turn the tables and invite the children to complete a "Report Card on the Teacher." If introduced carefully, and if assurances as to the intent are made clear, such a report card can provide insight for the students and valuable feedback for the teacher. The process briefly outlined below was implemented by Yves Parizeau in his fourth-grade classroom at Willows Elementary School in Victoria, British Columbia.

> **Children evaluate teachers.**

Mr. Parizeau first explained that he sincerely wished some feedback on his teaching, and that he wanted an honest and frank response. Guarantees of anonymity were given, and honored. A form such as the one in Figure 5–19 (p. 64) was presented, and students were reminded that there was no need for them to put their names on the forms unless they wanted to do so. Mr. Parizeau then suggested the qualities for which he wished feedback, asking the students to rate him on friendliness, fairness, and teaching. To ensure that the students had the opportunity to comment on qualities that they considered significant, they were encouraged to generate additional categories for themselves. Figure 5–20 (p. 64) is a composite list of the qualities the students deemed important. In order to obtain a personal rather than a group response, the students were asked to complete the report cards at home and return them the following day.

After the reports had been collected and read by the teacher, he made sure that the students knew he had carefully considered their comments and that he intended to make some changes as a result of them. It is important that students realize their comments have been taken seriously, and this can be handled without violating individual privacy. For example, one student noted on his form that he had particularly enjoyed a series of imagination exercises introduced early in the term and that he would like to do more such exercises. Without mentioning who had made the request, the class was informed of this and surveyed to see if they wished more exercises of that type included in the program.

> **Students appreciate being asked.**

MY TEACHER'S REPORT CARD

DATE: _____

CATEGORY	MARK	COMMENTS

Figure 5–19 **My Teacher's Report Card Form**

CHILD-GENERATED CATEGORIES

PERSONAL QUALITIES

- patience
- kindness
- niceness
- sense of humor
- considerateness

- temper
- physical fitness
- appearance
- effort

BEHAVIORS

- helping others
- helping with problems
- explaining
- encouraging
- organization

- speaking
- neatness in writing
- work habits
- riding your bike

CONDITIONS CREATED

- happiness
- homework
- field trips

- detentions
- interesting things

Figure 5–20 **Child-Generated Categories**

Mr. Parizeau found that the students reacted most positively to evaluating their teacher, as did those parents who commented on it. When it was first introduced, one student reacted with, "Oh, neat, *we* get to grade *you!*" They were all eager to repeat the exercise when it was offered again later in the school year. It is strongly recommended that this activity not be limited to a one-time-only trial; a great deal stands to be gained by inviting the evaluations at the beginning and toward the end of the year. (See Figure 5–21 for examples of reports completed by the same student over the course of the year.) If repeated, the students benefit from the additional experience in providing feedback, and the teacher has the opportunity to find out which areas concern the students, to make changes, and to obtain student reactions to the impact of the changes. One of the positive effects of this exercise was the contribution it made to the classroom atmosphere.

It takes courage for teachers to invite this type of evaluation. Children recognize and respect this, a fact that was evident in the care with which these reports were filled out. None of the students took the task lightly,

Risk-taking is rewarded.

A.

MY TEACHER'S REPORT CARD

	MARK	COMMENTS
FRIENDLINESS	A	—MR Parizeau makes me feel very comfortable and warm in the class. -He also trys to help out if there is a problem.
FAIRNESS	A	-I think that you are very fair to the class. Even if you give a detention you are being fair they deserve it.
TEACHING	A	-I think we do incredible things! example: We are not just talking about the Indians, we are doing things they did. example: having friends
LISTENING	B	-Sometimes Mr. Parizeau doesn't listen to you, but he usually does listen.
EXPLAINING	A	I think Mr. Parizeau explains very well, if you don't understand he will help you individually.

Figure 5-21 **My Teacher's Report Card: Two Examples. A: November 1987. B: March 1988.** (continued)

B.

	MARK	MY TEACHER'S REPORT CARD COMMENTS
FRIENDLINESS	A	-I THINK YOU ARE VERY " FRIENDLY TO ME; FOR EXAMPLE:YOU GREET ME WHEN I COME IN FOR CLASS. YOU SAY GOOD-BY BEFORE I LEAVE FROM SCHOOL. AND YOU SAY"THANK-YOU" WHEN I DO SOMETHING FOR YOU.
FAIRNESS	C+	-I THINK YOU COULD BE A LITTLE MORE FAIR WITH THE CLASS. FOR EXAMPLE: WHEN SOMEONE LOSES THEIR SPOT IN A BOOK WE'RE READING, THEY GET THEIR NAME ON THE BOARD (MAYBE SOMEONE WAS READING TOO QUIETLY AND THE PERSON DIDN'T KNOW WHERE WE WERE IN THE BOOK)
TEACHING	A	-I THINK YOU ARE A VERY INTERESTING TEACHER. OUR CLASS HAS NO WALLS. WE GO AND EXPLORE THE WORLD. I PERSONALLY THINK THAT'S THE ONLY WAY TO LEARN.
EXPLAINING	A	-I THINK YOU EXPLAIN THINGS TO ME VERY WELL. IF I OR ANYONE ELSE DON'T UNDERSTAND YOU WILL RE-EXPLAIN IT. YOU WILL EXPLAIN AND EXPLAIN TILL YOU UNDERSTAND.
ENCOURAGE-MENT	A	-YOU ENCOURAGE ME TO TRY HARD AND WORK HARD AND KEEP MY HOPES UP TO FINISH THE THING I AM WORKING ON.

Figure 5-21 *Continued*

and their comments were strikingly frank and considerate. While there were some suggestions for things the children wanted done differently, the comments also reflected a great deal of recognition, respect, and appreciation for many of the things their teacher was doing.

Chapter *6* ....

Gathering Information: Guidelines and Processes

. . . .

Report card time was fast approaching. As a beginning teacher, Marika A. viewed the prospect with mixed feelings. She was apprehensive about dealing with a daunting and unfamiliar task. Apprehension rose to near panic when she realized she had never actually been shown how to write a report card. However, she was confident of her assessment data. All term she had conscientiously maintained notes in her anecdotal notebook. Whenever the class was engaged in more or less independent work, she had observed and made notes. Minutes stolen at recess, lunch time, and after school had been devoted to recording noteworthy incidents in the recent past.

Finally, she sat down to review her notes. She began with Jason.

September 8:   Jason spent 20 minutes getting started.
September 11: Jason tipped his desk over.
September 12: Jason was asked by his cooperative
*   group to leave.*
October: Jason . . .
November: Jason . . .

Jason's trials and tribulations provided a rich resource of data on which to base bland summary judgements.

Jason has had some difficulties in adjusting to our classroom procedures. However, some signs of progress have been noted.

The next child on the enrollment list was Alan. Marika A. flipped through her anecdotal records. September, nothing; October, nothing; November, nothing. Clearly, a mistake had been made on the enrollment list. No child named Alan had been attending her class! But wait: the pale, whey-faced figure with lank hair who never spoke, rarely smiled. Third from the back by the window. That's Alan. What has he been doing all term?

· ·

Guidelines for Data-Gathering Procedures

This chapter deals with ways of collecting information that can be used in determining the extent to which children are deriving value from their education. Each procedure is exploratory and must be modified to suit the context in which it is used.

When devising or developing means of gathering information regarding various aspects of children's language performance, several guidelines should be observed. The tasks selected should:

- Use naturally occurring texts
- Use familiar language
- Proceed from the general to the particular
- Involve the (re)construction of meaning
- Require integrated behavior
- Be contextually grounded
- Appeal to children
- Generate implications for instruction

A naturally occurring text is one that was devised by its author for purposes other than language instruction or evaluation. There are two reasons for recommending this guideline. First, the teacher needs to know

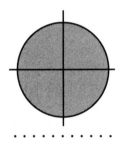

· · · · · · · · · ·

Data collection should be systematic and planned.

how well children can cope with real texts, real stories, real expositions, real arguments, or real poems. How useful is it to know how adept a child is at answering multiple choice questions based on very brief, artificially constructed paragraphs? Second, the study of language continues to uncover hitherto unsuspected dimensions. Recent examples include an increasingly sophisticated awareness of discourse, structure, coherence, cohesion, and the pervasiveness of metaphor that occurs in the language of all children. Early attempts to simplify written language for the purposes of instruction or evaluation were undertaken with no conscious awareness of these aspects of text. The results were inauthentic texts that required children to deal with them in inauthentic ways and that, in fact, made the task very difficult for them. Knowing how children deal with such texts will not necessarily tell us how they deal with naturally occurring texts. Tests that use artificially contrived texts are invalid because they do not measure what they purport to measure.

> **Real life belongs in the classroom.**

> **Simplifying text rarely makes it easier to understand.**

The need to use familiar language is related to the idea of the use of naturally occurring texts. Children learn best when most of the material is familiar. To ask them to read or write language that is unlike the language of life or of instruction is invalid.

A second reason for using familiar language is linked to our current understanding of comprehension. Comprehension can be thought of as the application of prior knowledge to a current situation. If children are confronted with inauthentic or peculiar language, then their capacity for applying what they know is reduced and their behavior is unlike the behavior they exhibit in normal language use or language-learning situations.

> **Naturally occurring language facilitates comprehension.**

The idea that development occurs from the general to the particular via a series of progressive refinements is a universal principle of language learning. Only those tasks that permit the learner to function in the same way will provide valid information for evaluation. Tasks that ask children to respond to minute details of decontextualized text do not reveal how students deal with real language situations.

> **Development proceeds from gross to fine.**

Normally, language users have one central purpose, which is the creation of meaning. All other considerations, such as sound/symbol association, grammatical complexity, spelling, and syllabication, are subsidiary. Consequently, all assessment tasks should involve the creation of meaning as a central focus. Furthermore, the act of creating meaning is constructive. In the case of speaking and writing, it is clear that language users are creating or expressing meaning. In recent years, many educators have come to appreciate that listening and reading are equally constructive.

> **Language is a constructive process.**

The listener or reader takes the incoming information and, using prior knowledge, creates a meaning from it. In this case, the term *reconstruction* is used because the meaning created must have some relationship to what was intended by the speaker/writer if communication is to occur.

Appreciation of the complexity of language, the constructive nature of language learning, and the application of prior knowledge makes it clear that language use and language learning are integrative acts. Reductive attempts to break language into simple parts and then to teach and test those parts may have been well-intentioned, but they were misconceived. While logical analyses of language and learning reveal the processes to be very complex (and thus seemingly too difficult for young children to manage), it is evident from close study of young children's language behavior that they thrive on complexity. Indeed, it may be that the complexity of language is due to the redundancy of interlocking linguistic systems that are vital for language to be learned at all.

Assessment procedures should be contextually grounded. Tasks employed during assessment should be as similar as possible to the tasks required during instruction and the demands placed on real people in real language situations. It is unreasonable to expect learners to behave in one way during instruction and another, for which they have not been prepared, during assessment. The issue is one of transfer. The degree of transfer from Task A to Task B is correlated with the degree to which Task B is like Task A. If assessment data is to be valid, then procedures used must be similar to instructional procedures.

Obtaining and holding the interest of children is an important feature of most instruction. It is well known that children learn more readily when they are interested than when they are not interested in the material. If motivation is removed from assessment, the behavior observed may not be like the behavior exhibited during learning.

Motivation is closely related to the notion of enjoyment. Existing testing procedures take motivation for granted. The child is simply asked to read a selection. Most children are very obliging. But no reason is ever given to the child for reading the selection beyond the implicit one of doing as the teacher says. The child has not chosen the passages because of an interest in the information that they convey. Invariably, the material is not relevant to the curriculum currently under study by the child. No problem is presented to the child. The behavior observed in a test situation will be much more revealing if the procedure sets the child an interesting problem to solve.

· · · · · · · · · ·

Language is complex.

· · · · · · · · · ·

Instruction and assessment are as a "seamless garment."

· · · · · · · · · ·

Motivation matters.

· · · · · · · · · ·

Tests as well as texts should be interesting.

Not every assessment procedure must meet every criterion. The more any given procedure approaches the ideal, however, the greater the degree of trust can be placed in the results.

Classroom Observations

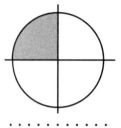

Classroom observations need to be focused.

The gathering of anecdotal classroom observations is not a simple task. The classroom setting is a dynamic one, with a large number of students involved in a great variety of activities, and teachers have many responsibilities in addition to recording observational comments. Because of such factors, there are two questions that commonly arise about gathering anecdotal observations:

1. How should an efficient record-keeping system be organized?
2. Which factors should be focused on evaluation?

Recording Anecdotes

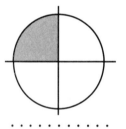

Record-keeping must be made manageable.

Classroom observation is an important source of information for evaluation. However, often there is no record to facilitate the comparison of observations over time, or to share with parents and students. A record of observations needs to be maintained.

One suggestion is to have teachers write down comments in a small notebook. Although many teachers have used this technique with success, many others have found that they carry the notebook frequently but write in it only occasionally. Even when the record is more extensive, this diary approach is prone to other problems. For example, when reviewing the record to report on student progress, it is often found that a few students predominate while others are overlooked. In addition, there is often no systematic focus to the observations. Experience with both novice and seasoned teachers shows that social behavior tends to be especially vivid and overrepresented in the record.

Records should be easily maintained.

An alternative to keeping a notebook involves the use of a large sheet of paper that is ruled into small squares, one for each student (see Figure 6–1, p. 72). This anecdotal collection page is kept in an accessible place in the classroom, ready to record the classroom observations of the teacher. Observations are recorded on sticky tabs, which are affixed to the master sheet in the appropriate place. These "sticky notes" are commonly available and can be easily attached to the record sheet. Such an

1. Rule a page in small boxes, one box for each student. Large size paper
    11 x 17 inches is ideal. A class of 32 can be accommodated if each box
    measures 2 x 2.75 inches. That is small, but sufficient for a brief
    comment.

    Make enough copies for each week of the school year, and use one
    page each week. Filling the page ensures one comment for each
    student.

Observation sheet for: _____ Focus:		John	Elizabeth	Paul	Leslie
		Jennika	Harpinder	Mirium	Wayne
Pansy	Caleb	Godfried	Galen	Andrew	Carol
David	Marika	Ty	Amber	Brondwyn	Laura
Natalie	Jason	Dennis	Jennifer	Peter	John

2. At the end of the week, clip out the comments and paste them into the
    student's personal file.

Figure 6-1 **Class Form for Recording Observations**

observation sheet has several advantages. First of all, it helps the teacher to ensure that each student in the class will have something recorded regularly, because as the student's boxes on the sheet are gradually filled out, the teacher's attention is drawn to students who have not yet had an observation recorded. Secondly, the space where the anecdote is recorded is small. This emphasizes the goal of regular, brief notes rather than extensive intermittent comments. The small writing space does not prohibit more extensive recording.

All students should be included.

Focusing Observations

What should the comments be about? There is usually so much happening in a class that teachers must be highly selective about what to record. Observations can be gathered in two ways: planned or spontaneous. Planned observations should be focused on a predetermined area of learning, and this can be signaled by the use of a key word.

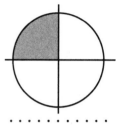

Both planned and spontaneous observations are informing.

A key word focus is easily incorporated into the class survey page procedure. The crucial question is, Where do the key words come from? Simply put, they come from the teacher. What do I want to know about the processes of student learning? What will the other stakeholders in the child's education want to know? The development of a set of key words will require selection on the part of teachers in consultation with other stakeholders. The starting point for this selection is the curriculum.

Key words cue observation.

The development of a set of key words from a curriculum document can be illustrated by using the British Columbia Language Arts Curriculum Guide as an example. This curriculum is conventional and thus is broadly representative of other curricula that might be encountered. The curriculum is organized around nine general goals, which are common across grades one through twelve. Each goal is further subcategorized into a series of objectives. For example, the first program goal is:

Observations are grounded in curricular goals.

> To develop the knowledge, skills, and processes needed to communicate effectively by listening, speaking, reading, writing, viewing, and representing.

There are five objectives listed for this goal. They are:

1. Set and identify purposes for communicating.
2. Communicate ideas with clarity and precision.
3. Experience satisfaction and confidence in the communication skills and processes.
4. Generate, explore, and extend ideas and information.

5. Read and view independently by choosing appropriate strategies and processes.

These objectives, while more concrete than the goals, are still broad. Nonetheless, each objective can be summarized by a key word or phrase such as *purposes, communicate ideas, confidence,* and so on. Thus, a teacher gathering information related to the first goal needs five key terms, one for each of the objectives.

The use of key terms ensures that the goals of the curriculum are being assessed. The task of deriving a set of observational key words from the curriculum is a way of simplifying the otherwise enormously broad task of selecting those aspects of students' performance which are relevant to the goals of the curriculum. Furthermore, the key words afford a frame of reference to help the teacher focus observations on processes and look beyond the more obvious features of social behavior.

Key ideas and words simplify the task.

Contextualized observations by teachers cannot be dismissed as subjective or in some way unreliable. Quite the contrary, the professional observations of the teacher who is intimately bound up in the classroom context are the most telling clues possible about the learning processes of a student. Adherence to the two principles of observation—observe in authentic situations, and observe for the purpose of interpreting learning processes—ensures the reliability of the anecdotal record of student performance. When these principles are practiced in the classroom and tied to the curriculum through appropriate sets of key words, there is every reason to be confident in the precision of observation.

Authenticity is one criterion of effective observation.

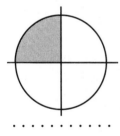

Checklists

Checklists assist in qualitative assessments.

Checklists are useful in two ways: they help to remind the teacher of what to observe, and they may also be used to inform other stakeholders what kinds of behaviors are valued. Numerous examples are available in the professional literature. However, other people's checklists are rarely as valuable as those developed by the teacher. The formulation of a checklist will help to clarify precisely what behaviors are indicative of successful learning in a given context.

The danger inherent in checklists is that they may act as blinders, producing tunnel vision. Teachers must remain alert to significant behaviors that may not be covered by the checklist. An example of a checklist is provided in Figure 6–2.

Pupil's name *Wesley*

Date	Activity	Chooses to join a group	Contributes to group discussion	Speaks confidently	Listens to others	Asks questions	Offers suggestions to another	Acknowledges others' contributions	Undertakes a task for the group
18/10	authors' circle	✓	✓			✓			
21/10	Japan project	✓	✓	✓	✓	✓	✓		✓
9/11	dramatizing-Novel		✓		✓		✓		
3/12	poetry booklet				✓			✓	
19/03	air band	✓		✓			✓		✓
5/04	science olympics	✓	✓	✓	✓	✓	✓		

Figure 6–2 **Checklist: Discussion**

Rating Scales

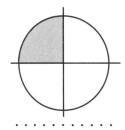

Rating scales have all the advantages and disadvantages of checklists. They have the added benefit of enabling the teacher to note the frequency or quality of a particular behavior. An example is shown in Figure 6–3 (p. 76). The added danger with rating scales is that the numerical rating invites summation across behaviors, resulting in an observational "score." Such a practice is unwise. It presupposes that the list of items on the rating scale is exhaustive and that each of the behaviors is of equal value.

Checklists and rating scales are best used to make qualitative rather than quantitative judgements. Both forms of data collection can be developed jointly with the children to whom they will be applied.

Rating scales indicate a measure of accomplishment.

Pupil's name: _____   Tony Martin   _____

Scale

5   needs to be extensively prompted
4   frequent prompting and repetition
3   occasional prompting and support
2   rarely asks for support or clarification
1   willing to take risks with minimal support

B O O K

	September Anne of Green Gables	October The Dog Who Wouldn't Be	November Code Red		
Comprehension					
retells with detail	5	2	1		
identifies main idea	3	1	1		
locates proof	4	2	1		
recalls ideas	3	4	1		
makes inferences	4	3	2		
justifies thinking	3	3	2		
Word Recognition					
reads fluently	4	3	2		
self-corrects	5	2	2		
uses context cues	4	1	2		
uses phonics cues	3	3	2		
applies structural cues	3	3	2		

Figure 6-3 **Rating Scale**

Assessing the Reading Ability of Individual Children

One of the most widely advocated means of providing in-depth information regarding reading ability is to create a structured oral reading and monitor the child's performance. Two of the most popular means of doing this are informal reading inventory and miscue analysis. In both situations, the child is presented with a series of unfamiliar passages and asked to read them at sight. While we do not reject these procedures entirely, we do have serious reservations about them.

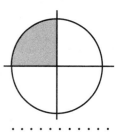

Many informal inventories are inauthentic.

Many informal inventories do not use naturally occurring texts. Particularly at the early primary levels, many inventories use the inauthentic language of the introductory levels of the basal reader. The reason for doing so is identical to the motive that produces "basalese"—a misconceived notion of difficulty level leads to the production of artificially controlled vocabulary and consequent loss of authenticity. Thus, procedures based on such texts produce behaviors for dealing with inauthentic language.

The inauthenticity of language leads to violations of other principles. The requirement that children read an unfamiliar form of language has a deleterious effect on their integrative behavior.

While miscue analyses are usually based on longer passages often selected from naturally occurring texts, one principle that is violated is the need for contextual grounding. This is particularly true for children who are introduced to reading by means of shared reading. During shared reading, the children receive modeling by an expert. They read repeatedly from a text which, if not already familiar to them, soon becomes so through repetition. Instruction occurs within a group whose collective voice is always ready to support or substitute should the individual stumble. In a miscue analysis and informal reading inventory, however, the learner receives no modeling. The text is unfamiliar, unrehearsed, and read only once. The task is executed individually. Thus, the means of assessment varies from the means of instruction. The discrepancies between shared reading and oral reading inventories are summarized in Figure 6–4 (p. 78).

Miscue analysis may not be contextually grounded.

The greater the discrepancy between assessment and instruction, the less faith that can be placed on the data generated from such procedures. This discrepancy was forceably brought home to us as we attempted to follow a group of six-year-old children through their first year of literacy instruction in a literature-based program. We interviewed each child in-

Assessment materials should be authentic texts.

Shared Reading	Reading Inventory
Modeling by the teacher	No modeling
Familiar text	Unfamiliar text
Rehearsal	No rehearsal
Group experience	Individual experience

Figure 6–4 **A Summary of Discrepancies Between Shared Reading and Reading Inventories**

dividually. Each was asked to read the current selection from an anthology and then from the introductory passages in a widely used, commercially available informal reading inventory. We were struck by the huge discrepancy between the joyful way in which children read their rehearsed texts and the halting manner in which they read the basal-like language of the unfamiliar passages. It seemed clear that any observations based on such behavior would have little relevance to how the children behaved in normal instructional sessions. As we watched them stumble through the unfamiliar material, all the behaviors common to "remedial" readers were noted: lack of expression, repetition, frowning, faces held close to the text, queries as to how much had to be read, and heavy sighs. It was clear that the assessment procedure was creating a high level of stress that was not evident when the children read familiar texts. At this point we seriously considered discontinuing the use of individual assessment. However, after much deliberation, we adopted and adapted an instructional procedure used by many teachers, which we termed text reconstruction.

Tests used in the early years of education often use "basalese."

Text Reconstruction

Materials Preparation

Reconstructing a text gives clues to process.

Select a short text that is likely to be orally/aurally familiar to the children but that is visually unfamiliar. Print each word of the rhyme on a separate card.

| Humpty | | Dumpty | | sat | | on | | etc. |

Procedure

Check that the text is aurally/orally familiar but visually unfamiliar. Ensure aural/oral familiarity by selecting a well-known rhyme ("Humpty Dumpty"). Check by asking each child if the rhyme is familiar. Be prepared to teach the rhyme to any child who does not already know it, or to try another rhyme ("Little Miss Muffet").

Present each child with the pack of word cards, which has been randomly scrambled. Tell the child that these are the words to "Humpty Dumpty," but that they have become mixed up. Ask the student to put the nursery rhyme back together again.

Data Gathering

Observe and record any aspects of the behavior that are indicative of the child's learning strategies, beliefs about the reading process, and levels of processing. From experience, we have developed a list of commonly observed behaviors and our interpretation of them.

Observation	Interpretation
Selects word without vocalization or hesitation.	Item is in the child's sight vocabulary.
Says "huh" while searching for *Humpty*. Correctly identifies the word.	Uses initial letter as word identification cue. Knows the sound value of the letter *h*.
Picks up *had*, says "horses," places it where *horses* should go.	Overuse of initial consonant as word identification cue.
Sets down *Humpty*. Says "Humpty Dumpty," moves on to look for *sat*.	Uncertainty over word boundaries.
Reads/recites text so far. Counts off words to identify the next word required.	Uses context to predict next word.
Sets lines of verse out in columns. Sets text out in one continuous line.	Uncertainty regarding text organization.
Fails to correct text that is upside down.	Is not yet using orientation as a cue to word identification.

The above list must be regarded as exploratory. The complexity of the reading process suggests that the list may be lengthy. The goal is not to develop an authorized list of reading behaviors, but to obtain some insight into how an individual child is processing text at a particular time.

Insight expands with experience.

The outcome of the text reconstruction procedure is not a level of performance, but a set of observations that can be used to compose a prose description of some of the child's reading strategies.

Interpretation

The behaviors observed can help a teacher build a picture of how the child tackles text. Individual behaviors can be interpreted as useful, not so useful, or missing.

Instructional Intervention

A need for instructional intervention, where necessary, is usually self-evident. If the children are unsure where the word *Humpty* stops and *Dumpty* starts, they can be shown. If the children are overusing *h* as an initial consonant, the words *had* and *horse* can be brought together and some means evolved (by the learner) for distinguishing between them.

Assessment should inform instruction.

Text reconstruction meets most of the principles listed above for data-gathering procedures. The reconstructive nature of the activity and the attitude of the children toward the task are worthy of note. The children are using their prior knowledge (oral/aural familiarity with the text) to solve the unfamiliar aspects of the task/text—the visual representation of the words. What is often most evident is the pleasure the children take in executing the task and their satisfaction in completing it.

Chapter **7** ·

Gathering Information: Products

The Assessment of Comprehension

Understanding and Meaning

Construction of meaning is the central purpose of language behavior. During instruction, the teaching of such things as word identification, phonics, and usage are subsidiary to understanding. In the process of language evaluation, the assessment of such variables as vocabulary size, reading miscues, spelling, and organization are secondary to the evaluation of the learner's capacity to construct meaning. It follows, then, that assessment of meaning is central to the evaluation of language.

Comprehension is taken to mean the procedure by which a person derives understanding. Meaning is not inherent in objects, situations, or texts but rather is assigned by persons as they seek to understand.

Current understanding of the nature of comprehension has rendered its assessment problematical. Reading comprehension results from the reader's application of prior knowledge to the information made available by the writer in an authored text. Listening comprehension is the application of prior knowledge to an aural/oral text such as a speech, lecture,

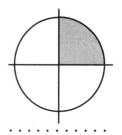

· · · · · · · · · · ·

Meaning is paramount in assessing comprehension.

reading, or sermon. Comprehension of mixed media such as picture books, movies, or television programs involves the application of prior knowledge to images, both moving and still; to sounds; and to messages spoken, nonverbal, and written.

Prior knowledge is the totality of what a person knows. It is the organized information inside the head, and roughly synonymous with terms such as *world knowledge, schemata,* and *long-term memory.* Prior knowledge results from our capacity to learn from experience. The degree to which every person's life experience is idiosyncratic, therefore, dictates the uniqueness of each individual's prior knowledge. On the other hand, the degree to which life experiences are shared produces commonalities of knowledge.

People in cultures that differ widely have fewer experiences in common, make different assumptions about the world, and tend to have communication difficulties when they meet. Students from mainland China, for example, are often puzzled by certain aspects of Western culture. They ask, What's Easter? Why isn't there a circus in Piccadilly Circus? What does it mean when it says that the captain was a "regular Captain Bligh?" and, What does "downing Coors" mean? These students can read the words but are not able to understand the cultural allusions, and therefore they do not fully understand the text.

> **Prior knowledge determines comprehension.**

Questions and Answers

It is the relative nature of prior knowledge that makes the assessment of comprehension difficult. If everyone's prior knowledge is to some extent unique, then the application of that knowledge to a text will produce an interpretation that is correspondingly unique. If the current practice of selecting a text and posing questions with single, definite answers is followed, then there arises the dilemma of whose questions and whose answers are acceptable. In framing questions, interpretive choices must be made. In determining the correctness of answers, the person who posed the questions must make value judgments about the responses. Whose interpretation of the text and whose judgment will be privileged? The paid representative of a commercial publishing company? A consensus from a distant and faceless committee? The child's? If all interpretations are acceptable, absolute relativism reigns, and evaluation becomes impossible.

> **Questions with single "correct" answers inhibit comprehension.**

Implicit in all educational measurement, and in many current attempts to assess comprehension, is an assumption that it is possible to measure a general capacity that applies across a variety of situations. The measurement of a person's height applies when s/he is playing basketball, dancing, swimming, or playing the flute. The same assumption is erroneously assumed to apply to a mental construct such as intelligence. A person with an IQ of 120 is assumed to be equally bright in all circumstances. It is clear that such is not the case. There are many situations in which highly intelligent people have acted foolishly.

There is more than one kind of intelligence.

The unsupported assumptions made about intelligence have been carried over to the assessment of language abilities. It is assumed that the measurement of a person's capacity to comprehend a specific text applies in all circumstances. This is simply not true. A reader's ability to understand a written text is largely determined by his or her background knowledge of the topic. It also depends on the reader's prior experience with texts of the type currently under examination. A reader may be adept at reading Dick Francis novels but at almost a total loss when confronted with a legal document, for example.

Resolving the Dilemma

One means of resolving the dilemma is to change the nature of the question asked when assessing comprehension. Traditional and current practice asks, Does the reader understand the passage? Implicit in this question is another, Is the reader's understanding of the passage correct? Correctness is defined as agreement between the views of the person posing the questions and the answers provided by the reader.

Does the reader understand the material?

An alternative approach is to ask, Does the reader have a reasonable interpretation of the passage? A reasonable interpretation is one in which the reader can cite relevant information from the text, and prior knowledge. Such an approach does not solve all problems. But it does recognize that there are a range of acceptable alternative interpretations to a given text. The question of who is to judge is not fully resolved. The people who judge "reasonable" and "relevant" are the primary stakeholders, in most cases, the teacher and child in consultation. Parents and colleagues may also be consulted if it is felt necessary.

Such an approach does not lend itself to fine-grained numerical scoring. Judgments tend to be made in broad categories, for example: Acceptable/Unacceptable or Excellent Justification, Adequate Justification, Poor Justification, Justification Lacking.

Judgments need to be made relevant to particular types of texts. Interpretations of fictional narratives, poems, and expositions would be

· · · · · · · · · · ·
**Different texts
require different
interpretations.**

judged differently. Summary judgments may need a prose commentary. For example:

> Josephine seems able to interpret the sequence of action in narratives suitable for her age range, but she is less able to explain the motives of characters.

Work Samples

The examples that follow are ways in which children can express their interpretations of texts. Each one reveals something of the child's understanding. In some cases, an oral or written commentary by the child provides an even greater depth of insight into the child's response. Each procedure is briefly described. Full explanations and examples are provided in Johnson and Louis (1987, 1990).

Reading: Reacting to Texts

· · · · · · · · · · ·
**Information used
should be
transformed
by the student.**

Children's reactions to text should always involve significant transformations of the information. The examples below are listed under transformation from text to image, text to text, and text to talk.

Text to Image

LITERARY POSTERS: Children make up a "Lost" poster for hopeful young protagonists who fail to return home, or "Warning" or "Wanted" posters for predatory villains who menace young protagonists.

LITERARY SOCIOGRAMS: Children make webs involving the main characters, objects, or localities and the relationships among them.

PLOT PROFILES: Children graph the rise and fall of tension and/or the fortunes of the protagonist as the story unfolds.

STORY MAPS: Children create a logical map of the landscape of the story and the movement of the characters across that landscape.

STORY GRAMMAR: Children arrange story events in a pattern that reflects the structure of the story. How the events relate to each other and how each relates to the theme of the story can also be represented.

ILLUSTRATION: Each child selects a scene described in graphic detail and renders it as accurately as possible as a picture.

Text to Text

LITERARY REPORT CARD: The child invents a reason for making a significant decision about a story character and then writes a school-style report on the character.

LITERARY NEWS REPORT: The child rewrites all or part of a story in the form of a news report.

COUNTDOWN: The child writes a series of clues about a concept selected from a text. The clues are arranged in ascending order of specificity. A second child reads the text on which the countdown is based and attempts to identify the concept after hearing or reading as few clues as possible.

CLUES: Children make up perplexing clues related to some concept in a recently shared text.

DIFFERENT POINT OF VIEW: Children retell a familiar story from the point of view of one of the minor characters.

· · · · · · · · · · ·
Many strategies can be used.

Text to Talk

In order to have a record of the following events, some form of media recording must be done.

LITERARY INTERVIEWS: Two children work together to plan a literary interview. One child adopts the persona of a character from a story. The second child plays the part of a media interviewer. The character is interviewed about events leading up to, during, and after the crisis presented in the story.

LITERARY PANEL: Characters from a story form a panel and are interviewed about the parts they play in the story.

LITERARY COURT CASE: Selected characters are brought to trial to face charges for misdemeanors and felonies. Similar treatment may be meted out to the authors of unsatisfactory texts.

When selecting student responses to text, care needs to be taken to ensure that the task remains an informing one for the student and the teacher. The activities just described above are all potentially rich and informing. Part of this richness is the diversity of the tasks. Sometimes even the best ideas can lose their power when they are overused and become routine.

· · · · · · · · · · ·
Assessment should be informing.

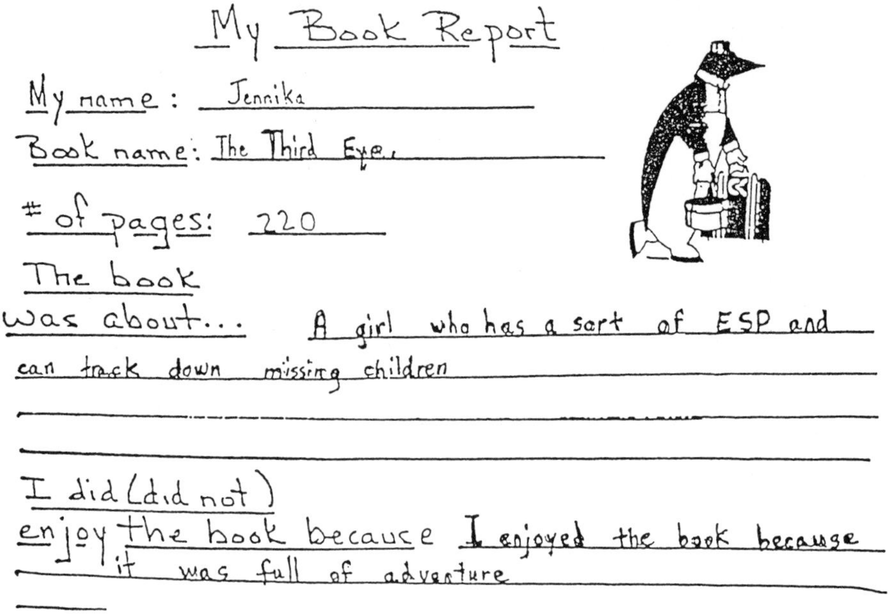
My Book Report

My name: Jennika

Book name: The Third Eye.

# of pages: 220

The book was about... A girl who has a sort of ESP and can track down missing children

I did (did not) enjoy the book because I enjoyed the book because it was full of adventure

Figure 7–1 **Routine Book Report File**

Recording should not become routine.

The fourth-grade student who produced the report shown in Figure 7–1 read over 300 books during the year and wrote a report for each one using the form which is illustrated. Nearly all the responses were repetitive, shallow, and typically classified the book as an "adventure," or as "funny." The largest number of books were summarized simply as "interesting" or "enjoyable." The task of routine form-filling produced routine responses. Even though the book report format was intended to elicit reflection by the students, it is clear this was not accomplished.

We suggest that teachers experiment with various approaches for gathering observational records of students' independent reading. The reporting tasks must encourage reflective reading. The information-gathering techniques should be varied. It has been found that keeping the collection of information simple enhances its value in evaluation.

Reflection leads to growth.

When the samples chosen to represent a child's growth have been identified, the child may be invited to add, in writing or on audiotape, reflective comments regarding his or her views on selection of past work, the progress perceived to have been made, and how past experiences have influenced present performance. Such reflective comments reveal the child's capacity for critical review, reflection, and self-evaluation.

Retelling: Predicting, Recalling, Interpreting, and Recasting Text

One straightforward yet powerful way to assess whether students are able to understand and reconstruct the meaning of texts heard or read is to have them retell the material. Retellings provide students with opportunities to synthesize, interpret, and personally recast the texts and stories to which they are exposed. When used as an assessment technique, retellings can be richly informative.

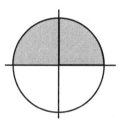

As Brown and Cambourne (1987) note, the procedure can be implemented in a variety of ways. The texts may be read to students or by the students. Retellings can be oral or written; they can be delivered to genuine or imagined audiences; and they can be individually or collaboratively undertaken. However handled, the basic task consists of having the student retell a selected text so as to convey as much of its content, significance, flavor, and impact as it is possible for the student to reproduce. Students are invited to retell the texts in their own words and in their own ways. This open-endedness grants them a measure of control over how they will display their understanding; they are free to report, highlight, and emphasize those things they consider most relevant and worth noting. In the process, a great deal can be learned (by both student and teacher) about how well the selected passage has been understood.

The instructional value of this procedure has been well-documented with students of various ages and abilities from widely differing cultural and social backgrounds (Brown and Cambourne 1987; Morrow 1989). Practice with retellings has been shown to result in greater oral language complexity, increased comprehension, enhanced awareness of the various ways different texts are structured, and increased utilization of literary language and genre-specific conventions. Only after students have become familiar with what is expected of them during a retelling, and have practiced and gained experience with the procedure, should retellings be used for assessment purposes.

Retelling reveals understanding.

If a particular retelling is intended to be retained for the student's portfolio, this should be discussed with the children before they read or listen to the target text. Similarly, they should be familiar with the type of text that is selected for the exercise and informed that they will be asked to retell the text before they begin reading. The following procedure, adapted from Brown and Cambourne (1987), is applicable when students are able to read the text for themselves and have sufficient command of written language to independently manage a written retelling. Although easily managed as a whole-class activity, it is recommended that students work in small groups of no more than four or five.

Cooperation enhances comprehension.

1. Each student is provided with a copy of the text, which has been folded so that the title is visible but the text is not.
2. Students are asked to read only the title and then briefly write their predictions about the likely content of the text. They can also be asked to predict and record specific words they might expect to find in a passage bearing this title.
3. Students are next encouraged to share their predictions with the other members of their group.
4. Each student is then asked to read the text and to assess the accuracy and appropriateness of the predictions made. Students should be encouraged to read the text as many times as they wish; it is important that they not be asked to begin their retellings until each one feels confident the text is fully understood. Students should be informed that the aim of the exercise is not to have them memorize the passage, but rather to have them retell it in their own words and in their own manner.
5. When each student decides he or she is ready, the text is put aside or turned over so that the print is not visible. Students are asked to retell—in continuous prose, pictures, or diagrams—the story or contents of the text in such a way that someone unfamiliar with it could enjoy, appreciate, or understand it. The particular instructions and recording format will vary depending on the purpose established for the retelling. For example, students might be asked to retell a narrative so that the motives of the characters are made clear. Before retelling an expository passage describing the life cycle of the monarch butterfly, they might be directed to emphasize the sequence of development. It is important that students be informed of the purpose of the retelling before the text is read, and that emphasis be placed on their ability to convey their understanding rather than on their spelling or penmanship.
6. Once the writing is completed to the student's satisfaction, s/he is asked to find a partner with whom to share and compare retellings. Students should be encouraged to note differences in the information included and the manner of telling, and to refer back to the original text to check omissions and questionable interpretations.

The purposes for retelling should be clear.

Two features that should be added to the above procedure are the provision of a genuine rather than an imaginary audience and the specification of evaluative criteria in advance.

Retelling can be used in assessment.

Retellings are primarily assessed according to how faithfully or reasonably the meanings and explanations reflect and interpret the original text. Naturally, the genre or nature of the text will largely determine the criteria by which its retelling is judged. Retellings of narratives are commonly rated according to how well they demonstrate awareness of story structure and include the relevant story elements and events. For example, questions that might be asked are:

1. Does the student appropriately introduce the story?
2. Is information about time and setting provided?
3. Are all of the characters included and appropriately described? Which, if any, are omitted?
4. Is the problem or plot correctly presented?
5. Are all of the relevant story episodes included?
6. Are the story events or episodes presented in the correct order, or in a reasonable and logical order?
7. Is the problem resolved and the story effectively concluded?
8. Is there any indication that the theme or point of the story has been appreciated?
9. Is the language or any stylistic device of the original reflected in the retelling?

Different criteria would be applied to the retelling of expository passages. Attention might be directed toward how clearly and completely the ideas and explanations are communicated, how effectively supporting detail is used, how accurately sequences or step-by-step procedures are replicated, and/or how logically arguments are outlined and supported. Obviously, the definitive characteristics of each different type of text would need to be reflected in the criteria used to assess the merits of its retelling. Retellings of poems or passages of dialogue would be judged very differently from those of either narratives or expositions. As suggested in a later discussion, much is gained if students are involved in determining the criteria for assessment.

Retelling is a procedure that is consistent with the general principles previously enunciated for data-gathering procedures. Natural language is used, and the reconstruction of meaning is paramount. Furthermore, integrated behavior is required, the process is contextually grounded, and implications for further instruction become evident. As well, the assessment of comprehension through retelling uses natural instructional activities as a basis for assessment and evaluation, and the procedure mirrors the way we display comprehension in real life.

It is true that evaluating a student's understanding of textual material through the use of retellings results in a qualitative judgment. However,

Data-gathering principles are honored in retellings.

when used over an extended period of time, observations about oral and written retellings can indicate growth both in understanding and in control of language. Furthermore, written retellings allow product assessment, which can be used to inform parents about their children's progress in reading and writing.

An added advantage of retellings is that they can be used for different genres in all content areas. Recasting information "in your own words" is both efficient and revealing, and it can result not only in an assessment of how well the material has been understood but also in whether or not the substantive content has been learned.

Reading: Student Record-Keeping

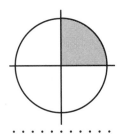

Reading logs provide an easily kept record of books read.

Students can also report to the teacher their own observations about learning. This can be facilitated in several different ways. In the case of personal reading, one of the simplest is to have students keep a personal reading log. Each time a student selects a book to read, it is listed on a record sheet such as the one illustrated in Figure 7–2. The information is easy for students to manage. This log would be used to list materials read during sustained silent reading as well as other self-selected reading. When one page is filled, the student begins another, and the completed lists are included in the student's evaluation folder. This simple technique reveals information on the scope of a student's reading. By surveying the list, a teacher can determine the range of topics that a student is reading as well as the frequency with which books are selected. Notice that this type of reading log does not include information about whether a book has been completely read or about the reader's reaction to a book. It is only a list of material selected. In order to monitor the development of reading and literacy in a more comprehensive way, other work samples are needed.

Writing: Negotiated Criteria

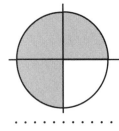

Criteria for judging children's work must be explicit and shared.

Students benefit when teachers make explicit the criteria by which judgments are made. In an open society, individuals should be as fully informed as possible about the ways in which they are to be evaluated. Evaluation should be as open as possible. It should not be done over the heads or behind the backs of children. The criteria for assessment and evaluation should be negotiated or jointly developed with the children during instruction. Such negotiation is one way in which the integration of instruction and evaluation can occur.

BOOKS/NOVELS YOU HAVE READ

	Title	Author
1.	Disneyland Hostage	Eric Willson
2.	MURDER ON THE CANADIAN	ERIC WILSON
3.	The twits	Dahl Roald Dahl
4.	The B.f.G.	Roald Dahl
5.	The ghost of Lunenburg Manor	Eric Wilson
6.	Time Machine	
7.	Flowers in the attic	V.C. Andrews
8.	Sweet valley high	Fransine Pose
9.	Sweet Dreams	
10.	Sweet Vally high	Francine Pascall
11.	Taffy Sinclair strikes again	Betsy Haynes
12.	Ghost hunter	Edward packcard
13.	The Voyage of the dawn Treader	C.S. Lewis
14.	Goasts Benith our Feet	Betty Wright
15.	Sweet Valley high	Franchine Pasco
16.	Ferret in the bedroom, Lizards in the fridge	Bill Wallace
17.		

Figure 7–2 **Record of Books Read**

Classroom Procedure

1. Identify the form of writing for focus (e.g., narrative, expository, persuasive, analytical, or argumentative).
2. Create or select three or four examples of the type of writing being considered. These samples should all be responses to the same task. They should vary in quality from unacceptable to excellent. The excellent example may be produced by an accomplished writer. For example, it may come from a published writer or the teacher. The other examples should, where possible, be produced by learners somewhat like the children to be instructed. Children have no difficulty in writing samples at various levels to bring out the desired teaching points.

Application of uniform criteria requires everyone working on the same tasks.

It is important that everyone is working on the same writing task. Otherwise the application of a uniform set of criteria is impossible. For example, everyone should be trying to persuade the school principal to take a particular course of action. Multiple examples are necessary because human beings learn through multiple, experiential encounters. Children learn what chairs, democracies, friendships, and lyric poems are by meeting many examples of these phenomena. Abstractions such as democracy or lyricism may need additional explanation, but numerous experiences with examples of a concept are necessary for learning to occur.

Multiple examples afford clarity.

Multiple examples are also required because the teacher plans to evaluate the children's responses. Consequently, it is necessary to convey to the children what constitutes good, acceptable, or unacceptable. What differentiates a good story ending from a mediocre one? When a novice author looks at a first draft, the questions become, How will I improve it? According to what criteria? Children need to be helped to derive specific criteria for judging quality.

One project (Rivalland and Johnson 1988) involved teaching fifth graders how to write persuasively. Small groups were given the task of defending the significance of selected fictional characters who were under threat of expulsion from their stories. Four teacher-generated samples of character defenses, based on the characters in "Little Red Riding Hood," appear in Figure 7–3.

3. Present the range of samples to the children and ask them to rank them. When rankings are suggested, seek justifications. If the first defense is better than the second, explain how. What makes it better? Record the gist of the child's response on the chalkboard. If the child says, "I prefer number one because it contains more information," then record "more information."

The Forest

I am where the story takes place. I represent the wide world that Little Red must deal with. Dangers hide inside me. If I was not in the story the wolf would have nowhere to lie in wait.

Wolf

I am very important. I have big ears and big eyes and big teeth. The woodcutter kills me. I try to eat Little Red.

Woodcutter

I rescue Little Red. If I were not in the story there would be no one to stop the wolf.

Mother

I am the quest setter. It is I who sent Little Red on her journey. It is I who warn her not to leave the path. It is I who tell her not to talk to strangers. It is when Little Red disobeys my cautions that disaster befalls her. It is through this calamity that young children learn to obey their parents.

Figure 7–3 **Examples of Character Defenses Based on "Little Red Riding Hood"**

At this stage, accept the responses of the children, even if they appear limited and, sometimes, contradictory. There are two reasons for this. First, it is desirable that the children evolve standards for themselves rather than have adult standards imposed prematurely on them. Second, the criteria are subject to review as the children acquire more experience with this form of writing.

> Children's responses should be accepted as they are.

4. Take one of the recorded comments and turn it into a rule. For example, the response "more information" might become the rule "The defense should include specific information about the character." Invite the children to turn the other recorded comments

into rules. Should rules become overly long, ask for short paraphrases.

There are two important characteristics of the criteria developed in this manner: The rules should be regarded as local and tentative.

Local rules mean that the criteria developed apply only to the form of writing under consideration. The principles that guide the composition of good stories are not the same as those that apply to good explanations. Further sets of guidelines are necessary for producing good arguments or effective persuasion. When teachers or textbook writers attempt to enunciate rules that apply to all forms of writing, they either retreat into unworkable generalities or focus on mechanical aspects. The former includes observations such as "Sentences should flow smoothly." There are many situations where this rule applies, but there are some where it does not. An author who is trying to convey uncertainty or indecision in one of the characters in a story might choose to use short, choppy sentences. No one set of rules applies to all situations and reasons people have for writing. Nor is there a rule to tell the novice when the rule does not apply.

Rules for spelling, punctuation, and grammar are more general in their application but even these are not universal. Authors who wish to convey dialect may effectively violate many conventions. Moreover, some teachers can reasonably be described as deficiency experts. Editing too easily becomes equated with error detection and correction. Teachers need to model effective practice. Effective writers revise first for substance. Novices focus too quickly on surface features. Teachers should help children look critically at the substance of what they have written. Concerns with mechanics take up increasing amounts of attention as the draft approaches "publication."

It is important that learners regard the criteria as *tentative* because no set of guidelines will deal with all situations. No matter how many examples or how long the list of rules that teachers present, the students will encounter situations that differ from those met during instruction. To deal with such situations, learners need to have internalized a set of adaptable general principles rather than a set of rigid rules. Consequently, teachers need to teach for flexibility rather than issue immutable edicts.

Tentativeness will be retained if students are required to develop their own criteria. Learners are aware of their own uncertainties and will recognize that present criteria are subject to future change. In contrast, if the teacher hands out rules, the children are inclined to regard these as immutable and universal, to be applied inflexibly to all situations on every

· · · · · · · · · · ·
Rules and criteria are always tentative.

· · · · · · · · · · ·
No single set of rules applies universally.

· · · · · · · · · · ·
Revise first for substance.

occasion. Such an attitude is pejorative to future development. The criteria developed by the children in a persuasive writing project are listed as items 1–4 in Figure 7–4.

Children develop
the criteria.

5. Give the children some guided experiences with the selected form of writing. In a persuasive writing project, the children revised the defense for the wolf and wrote a defense for the grandmother. In a descriptive writing project that involved providing detailed descriptions of dinosaurs, everyone practiced writing about the same dinosaur.

6. In discussion, have the class choose half a dozen of the best examples and evaluate the passages according to the negotiated criteria. Take the opportunity to revise or expand the criteria. If one or more of the samples is superior in a manner not covered by the agreed upon criteria, help the children expand the list appropriately.

Note that a *laissez-faire* approach is not suggested. As opportunities arise from the work produced by the children, be prepared to point out opportunities for refinement or extension of the criteria. The modifications suggested by the children in a persuasive writing project are listed as items 5–7 in Figure 7–4.

Aim for refinement
and extension.

7. Assign the children a writing task. This may be done individually or in a small group. For example, in another persuasive writing project, the children were put into groups of four. Each group

---

1. Must be based on facts from the story.
2. Must say the part of the character played in the story.
3. Must say why the part is important.
4. Must try to convince you
   a) why the character should be there,
   b) what would happen if the character were not there, and
   c) what is the use of repetition.
5. Arguments need to be in logical order.
6. Arguments should be based on as many details as possible from the story.
7. There must be a good final sentence that restates the main point or points.

Figure 7-4 **Criteria for Character Defenses**

was assigned a character from "Rumplestiltskin." One of the characters in the story was to be eliminated. Each member in the group was to write a defense trying to persuade the author to retain the assigned character. Any level of cooperative endeavor was permitted, but only one defense would later be selected at random to represent the entire group. In this way both individual effort and group cooperation were encouraged in order to make each defense as good as possible.

8. Require or encourage peer editing. Have the children share their work with their friends who, using the criteria, provide critical responses. Provide similar counseling yourself in individual conferences.

9. Hold a class discussion as to which character should be eliminated from the story. The least-adequate defense puts the character in jeopardy. Interestingly enough, sometimes defenses are so well-argued that a decision is impossible.

10. Using the developed criteria, provide diagnostic counsel and a numerical summation. Show the children which criteria have been met and which have not. Express the strengths and weaknesses orally in a conference, or in written comments. Finally, derive a numerical summation by counting how many criteria have been met and how many have not.

· · · · · · · · · ·

Peer editing is helpful.

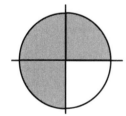

Writing: Work Required

Work required is a contract system widely used in Australia. It has been shown to have a beneficial effect on the atmosphere in the classroom, students' attitudes toward course work, and the quality of student work (Johnston and Dowdy 1988).

The contract in Figure 7–5 is designed for an upper-intermediate or junior high class. It presupposes a class set of the novel *Hatchet* (Paulsen 1988) and a class library of 30 to 40 books dealing with youngsters surviving alone in a hostile environment. The theme of survival is a very common one in adolescent literature. Teachers will have little difficulty obtaining sufficient material. Davis and Davis (1988) and Shapiro (1986) list more than 50 junior novels that address this theme.

When introducing the contract, the teacher may discuss with the class how the requirements and options might be legitimately interpreted. The class can be invited to brainstorm suggestions for each item. Suggestions might then be reviewed to determine practicality, availability of resources, and time constraints.

· · · · · · · · · ·

Requirements and options should be clear.

<u>Language Arts</u>

Unit: Survival Alone in the Wilderness

1.   Read <u>Hatchet</u>. Prepare a presentation that shows your understanding of the book.

2.   Record in your journal your thoughts as you:

     a)   read the book

     b)   prepared your presentation.

3.   Make your presentation to a small group. Record their reactions.

<u>Choose any two</u>

4.   Read at least three other books that deal with survival. Compare at least one with <u>Hatchet</u>.

5.   Interview at least one adult and one peer about survival in the wilderness. Write a report of the interviews. Include what you have learned as a result of conducting these interviews.

6.   Write one original survival story.

7.   Read three accounts of real life survival. Write your reaction to these articles.

8.   Self-selected survival project.

Figure 7-5 **A Work Required Contract**

Time constraints can be specified, negotiated, and renegotiated in the contract. However, it is difficult to predict exactly how much work can be done in a specified time. Loose time constraints may be imposed at first and tightened as teachers learn how much time a given contract might reasonably require.

Class members are presented with a range of directives and options. In many cases, assignments are open to interpretation. For example, the first item in the sample contract asks the students to prepare a presentation that shows their understanding of the novel *Hatchet*. It does not specify the nature of the presentation nor the nature of the understanding to be derived from the text. The teacher may leave the form of the presentation entirely open or limit student choices to a range of options. For example, the student may be allowed to select from the following list:

**Students define
their own contracts.**

- Make a plot profile
- Create a literary sociogram
- Make a map of the setting of the story
- Create a countdown for each of the major characters
- Create a "Wanted" or "Missing" poster for one of the main characters
- Write a literary report card on the central character

Each option would have been previously modeled through whole class instruction (Johnson and Louis 1987, 1990). Students need to be aware of the criteria by which each response will be judged.

The contract should provide opportunities for the student to engage in reflection on the processes in which they engaged while executing a task. For example, the second item of the sample contract requires the students to monitor their progress as they read the novel and as they prepare for their presentations. Ideally, journal entries should be modeled and discussed. If any form of response is acceptable, modeling is less necessary. The features of a good journal, however, should certainly be discussed by means of negotiated criteria.

**Guidelines are
provided.**

The contract should also provide opportunities for genuine communication to an interested audience. The third item in the sample contract directs the student to make a presentation to a group of peers. The assignment also asks the student to record the response of the group members, but it does not specify how this should be done. Jason, in Figure 7–6, has elected to make up a short quiz on his presentation.

**Genuine
communication
occurs.**

The options in the sample contract (Items 4–8) permit the student even greater freedom of choice. The eighth item is an entirely open-ended option. Jason has devised a project that involves the collection, interpretation, and presentation of data.

**Revision is part of
the process.**

Each item on the contract should be redeemable: that is, work that does not fulfill the contract may, at the discretion of the student, be revised and resubmitted. Written work may be submitted in its penultimate draft. If the draft is found by the teacher to be unsatisfactory, then the student is advised how to improve the work so that it meets required standards.

Jason Mulruiny

1.   I will do a character profile of the boy to show how

he changes.

2.   a) O.K.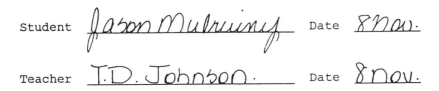

b) O.K.

3.   I will make a big chart of the character profile and

make up a 5 item test on my presentation.

Options

4.   I will read Island of Blue Dolphins, Tikta Liktak and

Call it Courage.   I will compare the central character

with the boy in Hatchet.

8.   I will present 10 members of the class with a list of

objects and ask them to choose which three they would

choose if lost in a northern forest.   I will present

the results to the class.

Student   *Jason Mulruiny*   Date   *8 Nov.*

Teacher   *T.D. Johnson.*   Date   *8 Nov.*

Figure 7–6 **An Example of a Child's Contract**

Advice on how to earn superior grades is given at the discretion of the teacher.

Reporting

The contract and the way it is negotiated by each individual student provides ample information upon which to report. Students who devise their own projects are likely to be risk-takers. Creativity, or its lack, will show up in the way students interpret the assignments. Planning, public speaking, and interpersonal processes will be evident in the small group presentations. The students' capacity to structure their own learning will be very clear in all phases of the project.

Writing: Selecting Samples

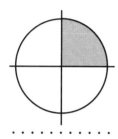

Work samples must be selected.

A questioning attitude reveals information.

Variety is an important element in assessment.

An important type of ongoing observation is the gathering of samples of student work for the purpose of evaluation. This gathering of work samples is the systematic selection of student products, which are retained for later reference in order to interpret and report on student learning. It is important to realize that examining a piece of work a student produced results in different observational information than observing the student in the process of creating a work sample. Suppose a student wrote a story extension at home after having read a novel. This piece of student work represents the end product of the writing process. While a skilled teacher may be able to infer something of that process, the actual learning activity behind the product is not evident. It is a familiar experience for a teacher to look at a student's product and ask, I wonder why s/he did that? The product itself does not necessarily inform the teacher. Of course, it is possible to reexamine the work sample at a student-teacher interview, in which case additional information about the process behind the product becomes available.

Students who are actively involved in learning create a wide variety of products. It would be burdensome for teachers to attempt to gather examples of every type of work. Also, the resulting files would be so massive that the identification of important features of development could be hidden. In order to ensure that the portfolio of student work samples provides information about both the student's individual progress and the curriculum that the student has been experiencing, it is essential that the selection of products be deliberately limited.

Writing Folders

One source for student work samples is a writing folder. The use of student writing folders has become a feature of many classrooms. Figure 7–7 illustrates two different organizations that such folders could use.

The writing folders represent a rich resource from which examples of actual student work can be drawn for inclusion in an assessment portfolio. The selection is not simply for the purpose of demonstrating a student's "best" work. Rather, the samples are to reflect the ongoing

A.

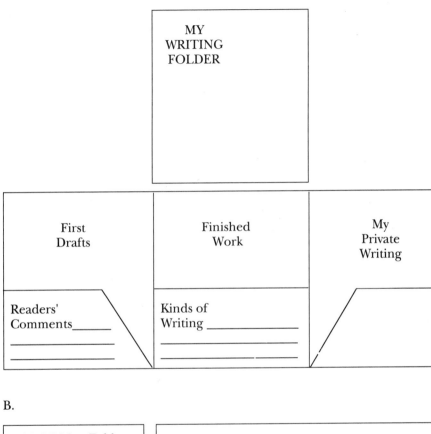

B.

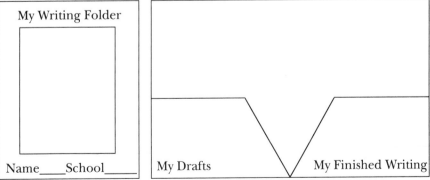

Figure 7-7 **Writing Folders (from Woolings 1984). A: Junior/Intermediate Folder. B: Primary Folder.**

development of a number of aspects of writing. For this reason, it is essential that not only the polished versions of student writing be included, but also initial ideas and drafts. For example, an initial collection of impressions and a subsequent ideas web would reflect the student's use of organization in writing. Initial drafts with revisions scribbled over them indicate the use of editing.

Drafts as well as final products should be evaluated.

The selection of examples of student products should not be restricted to personal and "creative" writing, but should include samples of writing from other areas of the curriculum. Atwell (1990) lists 30 different genres for report writing. Her list includes textbooks, correspondence, journals, scripts, autobiographical sketches, poetry, science fiction, how-to books, field guides, recipes, games, catalogues, family trees, bulletin boards, choose- your-own adventure stories, time lines, calendars, alphabet books, and annotated dioramas. While many different genres are experienced in the classroom, the evaluation portfolio should reflect those genres that are experienced repeatedly and thus offer the best opportunity to reveal development.

All content areas should be included.

The child's writing folder may include written material, images, and recordings of oral responses. The entire collection should reflect the balance of the program. If the program has emphasized experience with expository texts, for example, then this form of text should predominate in the writing folio.

Balance is important.

The selection of samples of student writing products could be done by the teacher, the student, or both together in consultation. In this way, the selection not only represents various aspects of the writing process, but also reflects the student's judgment. The following are suggestions for inclusion.

Students should be included in the selection process.

WRITTEN MATERIALS: Written materials should be reflective of both process and product. All samples should be dated and reviewed chronologically.

SAMPLES FROM THE CHILD'S LEARNING LOG: Samples taken over time can be used to demonstrate development in a particular area. Each sample entry may be regarded as a product, but the changes over time will show aspects of process.

SAMPLES OF THE CHILD'S PUBLISHED WORK: Published is defined by classroom practice. Publishing may mean reading aloud to the class, posting on the bulletin board, sending home, placing in the school library, or some other way of sharing with a wider audience.

SAMPLES THAT DOCUMENT THE DEVELOPMENT OF PUB-LISHED WORK: Such samples might include initial jottings of exploratory ideas, research notes, first drafts, intermediate drafts, and final drafts.

SAMPLES OF WORK PRODUCED IN CLASS, EXECUTED AT HOME, AND PRODUCED INDIVIDUALLY: For example,

Expository reports: Factual explanations or descriptions of some aspect of the real world.

Critical reviews: A critical review of an experience, media presentation, stage play, or written text.

Narrative: Personal or fictional narrative.

Journal entry: Samples of journal entries.

Creative responses: There are a very large number of ways in which children respond creatively to text (Johnson and Louis 1987, 1990), and examples should be included in the student's profile of achievement.

Chapter 8 ·······················

Interpretation

Questions to Ask of the Data

Up to this point in the evaluation cycle, the focus has been on collecting information about students. A general organizational framework for gathering data (the Quad) has been described, and a number of data-gathering procedures outlined. Simply gathering information, however, is only one part of the evaluation process. What is of greater interest to teachers, students, and parents is what the information means. What does it tell about the learning that is taking place? How can we summarize a wide array of information in a coherent and accurate statement to share with others?

·········
Interpretation of data has received little attention in the literature.

Making Judgments

The teacher faced with the need to interpret information about the class is in a situation like that facing any researcher. The conclusions can never be better than the data on which they are based. Therefore, the key to interpretation is to have a rich source of information from which to work. For the classroom teacher, this information is pro-

Initial judgments are hypotheses which must be confirmed or rejected.

vided by day-to-day interaction with students and by placing a selection of these experiences in the student data profiles. Each profile affords the possibility for a number of different interpretive hypotheses. But that does not mean that every hypothesis is as good as every other one. Some have greater educational consequences than others. Teachers are wise to focus on those aspects of literacy that are critical to further learning. For example, concern about comprehension takes precedence over phonic minutiae.

Judgments must be data driven.

On a day-to-day basis, teachers have a set of intuitions about the students in their classes. Formulating a judgment, however, involves more than simply recording an intuition. It is crucial that we confirm the intuition. There are two basic ways of accomplishing this when reviewing data profiles: looking for convergences and looking for divergences. For example, suppose that a fourth-grade teacher has a hunch that a student, Amy, needs help in reading because she does not understand sound-symbol relationships. In Amy's profile, there are notes that document her halting oral reading. Elsewhere in the file, however, there is a draft report that shows broad word choice and accurate spelling. There is also a sample of poetry that shows inventive language like "grog" for green frog and "snegg" for a snake's egg. While Amy's oral reading may confirm the hypothesis of confusion, the writing evidence suggests that Amy has control of the orthographic system. There is reason to be suspicious of the original hunch because of the incompatible data. Therefore, it would be wise to check further before making a judgment.

Fundamentally, a judgment about a student is only an hypothesis, the accuracy of which is limited to the amount and quality of information gathered.

The general process for forming an interpretation is:

1. Gather discrete findings.
2. Cluster the findings into related sets or patterns.
3. Describe the general character of these sets or patterns.
4. Review the portfolio for corroborating evidence.

Judgments about children are always tentative.

Above all, it must be remembered that interpretation needs to be done cautiously. Judgments can be consistent and still be wrong. Miles and Huberman (1984, 6) report that Einstein concluded, "No amount of evidence can prove me right, and any amount of evidence can prove me wrong." A judgment about a child must always be regarded as tentative not only because of the difficult challenge of formulating insightful judgments, but also because children change with great regularity.

Interpreting Language Growth

Before data are interpreted, judgments made, and parents informed, it seems necessary to examine once more the nature of language growth. In fact, the evaluations we make depend on the perspective adopted. Descriptions of growth in literacy often rest on unexamined metaphors such as movement along a continuum, progress along a track, or climbing to a "higher" level. Common to all these views is the idea of a fixed sequence through which the individual, seen as a moving point, is expected or required to pass. This notion of linearity is often expressed visually as a track (Figure 8–1a, p. 108) or a staircase (Figure 8–1b). The learner makes progress by moving along a predetermined pathway. During language arts instruction, this is very often manifest in the form of a basal reader and sometimes characterized by levels. During evaluation, the track is formed by the items on a standardized reading test.

Implicit in the moving point metaphor is the idea that time equals distance. When rate enters the equation, the continuum of growth then becomes an agenda—a certain amount of material is to be covered within a given amount of time. If children are said to be "behind," it is this implied agenda that sets the desired pace. We must then consider who determines the agenda. On what basis? And for whom?

Language does not develop in a linear fashion.

The agenda should not be narrowly fixed.

Language: Observed and Measured

If, on the other hand, instead of using a predetermined continuum we symbolize an individual's language capacity as a circle, then a circle representing a one-year-old child would be small because the language repertoire of an infant is small. Cooing, eye contact, crying, body language, and the use of a few single words that relate to the immediate present would be characteristic communication strategies. It is very difficult to learn from a one-year-old what she or he thought of the sunset you both saw last evening (Figure 8–2, p. 109).

If we symbolize the individual's language capacity one year later, then we must use a bigger circle to reflect the increase in the child's repertoire. It must be recognized that the two-year-old has not lost or left behind the one-year-old repertoire. At two years, the child can still coo, maintain

Language growth is cumulative.

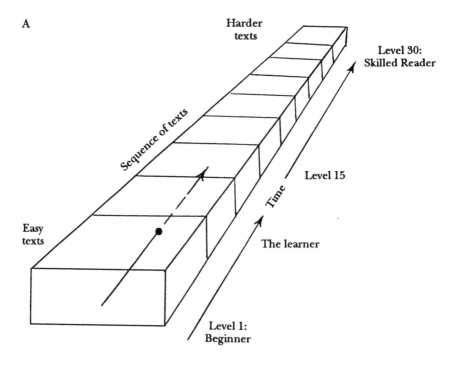

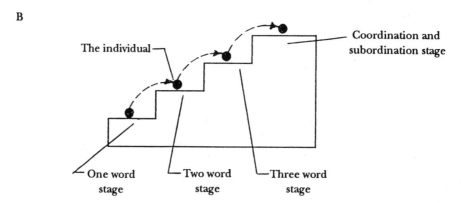

Figure 8-1 Linear Views of Language Acquisition. A: Track. B: Staircase.

eye contact, cry, use body language, and say single words. The change can be symbolized by adding a second concentric circle (Figure 8–3). Thus, language growth is seen as the development of an expanding repertoire, which may be symbolized visually as a series of concentric circles (Figure 8–4). The contents of an individual's language repertoire are heavily influenced by culture and experience. A child raised among adults who speak in a dialect will adopt that dialect. The contents of the language repertoire are all highly interrelated. The capacity to read well may enhance one's capacity to write. A large oral vocabulary will aid in the

An expanding repertoire of language is the goal of instruction.

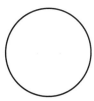

Figure 8-2 **Language Repertoire at One Year**

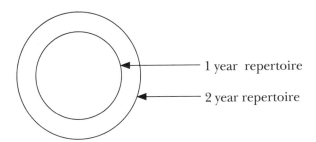

Figure 8-3 **Two-Year Repertoire**

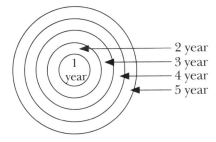

Figure 8-4 **An Expanding Repertoire**

All aspects of language are interrelated.

development of a written vocabulary. The components of the child's language repertoire tend to develop together. Increases in reading ability may be reflected in writing. Such connections are not universal, however, because one can find cases of children with advanced oral skills who, despite instruction, are barely literate.

If language growth is the development of an expanding repertoire of abilities, why do language studies keep reporting growth as linear? The answer is that linearity is an artifact of the measurement process.

When language is measured, the window is very small.

Language is too complex for any one researcher to measure all aspects of an individual's language ability. Consequently, choices must be made. The researcher selects one feature of language. Assessment, then, is not conducted on language but on some aspect of language. If growth in oral language is the focus, then one or two features of oral language, such as the use of prepositions or the formation of plurals, is chosen and measured over time. The following points should be noted:

1. At the time of the first sampling of the child's language behavior, the child has a language repertoire that contains many other features other than those selected by the teacher.
2. At the time of the second sampling, the child's language repertoire will have grown in many ways other than those that are the focus of the assessment. The changes in the selected features may be affected by changes in other language capacities that fall outside the focus of the teacher.
3. Language growth continues to proceed in a dynamic, holistic fashion. The language feature selected for study is only one aspect of the changes that occur.

When the assessment period is over, the researcher reviews the information and tries to make sense of it. But the information is limited only to those features of language that were examined. In a linear model, the full panoply of complex behaviors and the ways in which they interrelate are not considered. In an holistic model, however, a perception emerges of a complex human being coping more or less effectively in a number of situations that vary in both space and time. The focus is on the changes the learner is undergoing rather than on arrival at some point along a fixed scale.

Evaluation looks at change.

Up to this point, the child's language repertoire has been symbolized as a circle; growth has been idealized in the form of a series of concentric circles. In reality, however, actual language growth is not nearly so tidy. The circles are more representative of an idealized age-based expectancy. A circle labeled five years represents the repertoire of language we normally expect from a five-year-old. But our expectations are not fixed. We also anticipate variation across individuals. A group of five-year-olds will manifest a wide range of language performance. Thus the boundaries of the circles must be fuzzy. There is no fine line that separates the five- and six-year-old (Figure 8–5).

Nor does any actual individual uniformly conform to our specific age-based expectations. In some areas, growth may be less than expected. In others, expectations may be exceeded (Figure 8–6, p. 112). The extroverted child may have well-developed oral language, limited capacity for reading, and very poorly developed ability in writing. The shy child, inept in verbal abilities demanded in social situations, may become adept in both reading and writing.

Furthermore, growth does not occur evenly on all fronts. We voluntarily practice that at which we excel and avoid those things that are difficult. A child who receives attention and commendation for being social is attracted to social situations and rapidly develops the verbal skills required in such contexts. The shy child who shuns group involvement falls further and further behind. Thus, language growth is more adequately represented as in Figure 8–7 (p. 112), where in some areas the seven-year-old's language falls into the expected range, in others it is more like that of a six-year-old, and in still others it has the features of an eight-year-old's. From this example, it is easy to see why it is essential to gather information about as full a range of a child's repertoire as is possible. Otherwise, the assessment will result in a distorted view, and the evaluation will not be truly representative of the child's language growth.

· · · · · · · · · ·
Variation occurs between and within individuals.

· · · · · · · · · ·
Growth is never symmetrical.

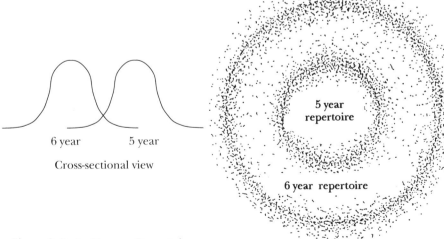

6 year   5 year

Cross-sectional view

5 year repertoire

6 year repertoire

Figure 8–5 **An Uneven Repertoire**

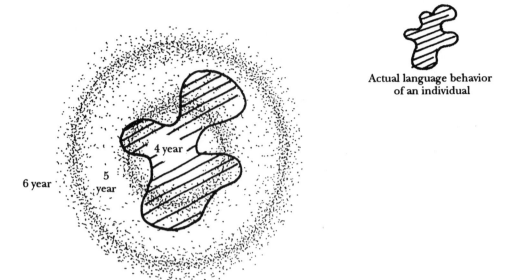

Actual language behavior
of an individual

Figure 8–6 The Language Repertoire of a Four-Year-Old Child

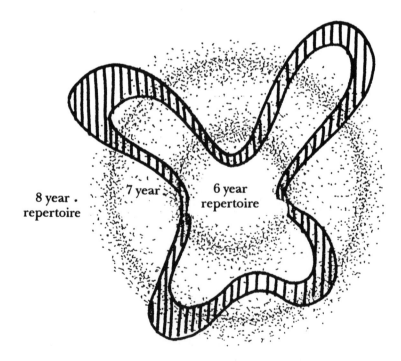

Figure 8–7 The Language Repertoire of a Seven-Year-Old

Individual, personal experiences as learners; experiences with children; and a plethora of research findings over the past 20 years leave no doubt that a linear view of language development is simply not justified and should not be used as a basis for measurement in assessment and evaluation. Rather, an holistic perspective should be adopted and should form the basis of literacy and language assessment and evaluation.

Much of the perspective offered in this book thus far can be summarized by the diagram shown in Figure 8–8. Information for assessing and evaluating the child's capacity for language and literacy is provided by the three major stakeholders: the child, the parents, and the teacher. The information may take three forms: anecdotes based on observations,

· · · · · · · · · · ·

Holistic views reflect the richness and complexity of language development.

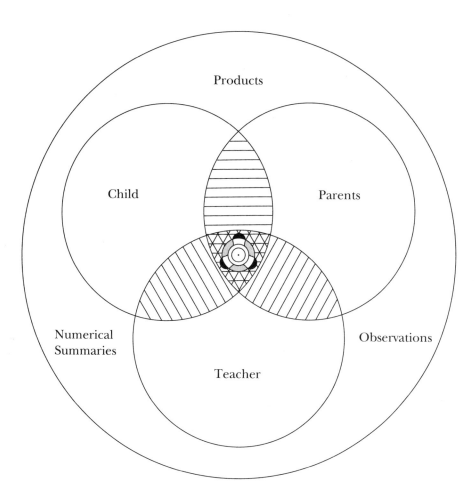

Figure 8-8 **Assessment and Evaluation**

examples of the child's work, and numerical summaries (either contextualized or decontextualized, as depicted in the Quad). The significance assigned to any one of these types of information will differ with each individual circumstance.

Information is collected in order to develop an adequate description, interpretation, and evaluation of the child's language repertoire. Incremental growth in the repertoire is symbolized by a series of concentric circles. The range of normative expectations for any given child is represented as a speckled band. The fluctuating achievements of the child are represented by an uncertain area that expands idiosyncratically on a multiplicity of fronts. Achievement that falls significantly above or below expectation is shown in patches of solid black. Such areas would be addressed in written reports and face-to-face conferences.

The entire procedure is encircled to symbolize the holistic nature of the endeavor.

Chapter *9* . . . .
Evaluation in an Integrated Classroom

The Grid

In order to successfully integrate and evaluate across the curriculum, a change in perspective is required. Listening, speaking, reading, writing, and viewing must be considered as processes, along with other such processes as risk-taking, reflection, and problem solving. The language arts are not to be viewed simply as subjects to be taught but instead as means through which the content subjects are explored. This idea can be roughly conceptualized as a grid, as in Figure 9–1, p. 116.

It is not expected that the teacher would necessarily monitor all of the spaces designated by the grid. Rather, it is recommended that the teacher select a representative sampling that would fairly reflect various processes in the context of at least one of the different subject areas. Thus in evaluating achievement, one might think in terms of reading in social studies, for example, or writing in science. A teacher might consider oral language proficiency in a social studies research project, or the ability to verbalize a concept in mathematics. The possibilities are endless—the point is, however, that reading, writing, listening, speaking, and viewing are no longer decontextualized but are integrated into the substantive work being undertaken in the class.

. . . .

An integrated curriculum requires a change in perspective about evaluation.

. . . .

Selection is necessary.

CONTENT AREAS

	Literature	Science	Social Studies	Art	Mathematics	Music	Physical Education
Reading							
Writing							
Speaking							
Listening							
Viewing							
Spelling							
Risk-taking							
Monitoring							
Reflection							
Problem Solving							
Evaluating							
Decision Making							
Collaboration							

(Left margin labels: STRATEGIC PROCESSES)

Figure 9–1 **The Grid**

Very much the same sort of notion applies to the language arts themselves. All are integral aspects of a literacy acquisition process and should not be artificially separated in order to be addressed. When reading to children, for instance, we are helping them with their writing and introducing them to an expanding repertoire of written language forms.

· · · · · · · · · ·

The language arts are interrelated.

Perhaps an even more important point has to do with the fracturing of language into so-called subskills. For purposes of assessment and evaluation, it makes no sense to focus separately on such areas as phonics, spelling, usage, punctuation, and so on. Children learn language in meaningful, holistic, contexts progressing from whole to part or from gross approximations of standard use to finer and finer refinements of linguistic form. Students should be evaluated on their developing abilities to "make meaning" or effectively orchestrate the language—that is, to appropriately transact meaning with someone else in one form or another. Information about subskills is useful only when it provides insight into the student's ability to communicate effectively. As far as assessment and evaluation are concerned, the end in view is to develop a profile of achievement: a documented record of growth that will show for each individual the progress being made and allow for effective, purposeful evaluation.

In considering the language arts as a unified whole that facilitates growth in all areas of the curriculum, educators are beginning to understand the true nature of integration. By focusing assessment and evaluation on the ways in which language is used in a variety of content areas and learning situations, a multidimensional, valid, and reliable record of accomplishment is achieved.

The term *strategic processes* has been used to embrace those activities that apply across a range of curriculum areas and a variety of situations. Of course, there is overlap in these processes (for example, risk-taking plays an important role in reading). The suggestion is, however, that all the behaviors listed in Figure 9–1 can be noted in a wide variety of circumstances. Children demonstrate their capacity for oral expression, for example, in all areas of the curriculum. Similarly, risk-taking, monitoring of ongoing behavior, and reflection are evident in each academic area and in a variety of social situations.

Strategic Processes

It is important that teachers experiment with the collection and reporting of data on strategic processes such as risk-taking, self-monitoring, and reflection because these strategies are causative factors in successful learning. They also have clear implications for instruction. A child who is unwilling to take risks is in need of assistance. Children who do not monitor their own behavior require help. The unreflective child is at a disadvantage. Teachers should not assume, however, that the absence of a desirable process is due to a deficit in the child. A child may be reluctant to take risks in a classroom environment because caution and conformity are consistently rewarded and also because mistakes are pun-

Subskills serve meaning.

A profile of achievement indicates growth.

The record must be multidimensional.

Strategic processes should be noted.

Reflection should be encouraged.

ished. Adjustments may be necessary in the ways in which children are encouraged to behave. A lack of monitoring and correcting one's ongoing behavior during reading or writing, for example, may be due to ignorance. Some children may simply not realize that this is what they are supposed to do. Demonstrations, discussion, and encouragement of monitoring behavior should occur.

As important as these processes are, the challenge facing teachers is how to identify them. The following are some exploratory indicators:

. . . .

Self-monitoring is important.

Risk-taking During Discussion

. . . .

A secure environment is necessary to encourage risk-taking.

- Willingness to participate in public events that require spontaneous reactions (for example, panel discussions, debates, interviews)
- Offering novel solutions to problems
- Offering multiple solutions to problems
- Sharing personal concerns or fears
- Volunteering to undertake responsibilities
- Willingness to adopt an unpopular role or position
- Offering original interpretations of texts
- Willingness to speak in a large group
- Willingness to argue with the teacher

Risk-taking When Reading

- Reading a wide variety of topics and authors
- Skipping unknown words and reading to the end of the sentence in order to identify meaning
- Using context to approximate the meaning of an unknown word
- Willingness to accept an approximate meaning of an unknown word
- Willingness to continue reading an entire text even though every word is not understood
- Predicting outcomes

Risk-taking While Writing

- Using approximate spelling of unknown words
- Experimenting with punctuation
- Experimenting with writing styles
- Writing in a variety of genres
- Borrowing and adapting writing techniques learned from reading experiences

- Interpreting assignments in a creative manner
- Seeking permission to reinterpret assignments

Monitoring and Self-correction During Discussion

- Willingness to modify an expressed position in the light of new information or superior reasoning
- Ability to detect a logical fault in one's own argument
- Ability to draw inferences
- Self-correcting mispronunciations or grammatical errors
- Commenting on the effect of one's own contribution to a discussion

Self-correction spurs growth.

Monitoring and Self-correction When Reading

- Self-correcting miscues when reading aloud
- Expressing puzzlement or confusion when a text does not appear to make sense
- Expressing changes in attitude toward a character who undergoes development in a story
- Asking questions of a text and then searching for answers
- Checking predictions made earlier and modifying them in the light of new information

Monitoring and Self-correction While Writing

- Voluntarily reading and editing drafts
- Expressing dissatisfaction with the effect of a draft and the original intention for writing it
- Asking others to listen to a draft read aloud
- Actively seeking advice on early drafts
- Anticipating audience reaction and modifying drafts accordingly
- Talking to self while writing, editing, or proofreading

Reflection While Writing

- Expressing opinions and thoughts about the day's events in a journal
- Offering arguments on paper (for example, presenting two or more points of view on an issue)
- Providing support for critical appraisal of one's own writing
- Providing support for critical appraisal of one's own progress in writing over time

Reflection During Discussion

- Asking reflective questions (for example, I wonder why? . . .)
- Asking questions about "obvious" phenomena (for example, Why does it get dark at night? Where does the wind go? Where does Santa Claus go to the bathroom?)
- Asking others how they arrived at conclusions

Reflection When Reading

Readers often reflect while they are reading but the process is likely to be entirely covert. However, reflection can be inferred by overt behaviors as follows:

- Talking and writing about texts read
- Relating texts read to personal experiences
- Relating texts read to a personal value system
- Providing support for critical summation of texts (for example, ability to justify an evaluative opinion)
- Providing support for critical comparison of current text with previous reading
- Perception and appreciation of irony, parody, and sarcasm

Reflection is a covert process.

The covert nature of reflection means that it is not readily observable. However, valuable information can be obtained by means of an interview or a questionnaire. Children who are reflective will be able to express more of what they are thinking about as they read, write, and observe across all curriculum areas.

Information on strategic processes has a higher utility and wider generality than an attainment level or a grade in a content area such as social studies or science. It is possible to live a fulfilling life without learning the major exports of Idaho, for example, but anyone unable to take risks may well be hampered in many aspects of life.

Strategic processes are not abstractions.

Rather than talking and thinking of strategic processes as abstractions, teachers should discuss them as they are exemplified in various areas of the curriculum. Risk-taking may be noted in social studies, art, or mathematics. General evaluative summations should be based on multiple observations in several content areas. Risk-taking should not be confused with imprudence or foolhardiness. The calculation of risk should take into consideration the benefits of success and the consequences of failure. In some areas, teachers have some control over the consequences. A child whose experiment with a new genre does not succeed should be commended for courage. But in an area such as industrial arts, for example, mature prudence must prevail and where necessary, be imposed. Risk-taking with a band saw could be fatal!

It is clear that information on risk-taking, monitoring, and reflection will not be available unless the children are provided with opportunities to engage in such strategic processes. Children will not express a capacity for reflection, for example, if they never have the chance to be reflective.

The concepts risk-taking, monitoring, and reflection are not autonomous or separate. The monitoring of a current situation and reflection on how it compares with similar situations in the past will affect the nature and degree of risk one is prepared to take. Monitoring and reflection are not always clearly separable. Monitoring usually refers to a measure of self-awareness as speakers, readers, or writers observe their ongoing behavior. Reflection is most clearly evident when one thinks back over an experience. If monitoring can be thought of as working on a microscale, then reflection works on a macroscale. However, drawing an inference represents an intermediate case. If one is reading a detective novel and notes that the murder was committed at night but the dog didn't bark, then one is monitoring the information provided but reflectively relating it to world knowledge (a dog would bark at a stranger) to make an inference.

The grid presented in Figure 9–1 is a practical way for teachers to evaluate in an integrated classroom. If we are to pay more than lip service to the concept of integration, then we must also evaluate in an integrated way.

The environment must be rich in opportunity.

Making inferences enhances comprehension.

Chapter 10

Issues That Won't Go Away

. . . .

Jeremy had a long history of slow progress and lower-than-expected performance. For the preceeding three years he had received grades of C or C— in language arts. During the past year, however, he had demonstrated a marked improvement in motivation and progress. He was reading on his own with material that was generally suitable for younger children. He had rigorously undertaken a science fair project that needed substantial support for presentation. For the first time, he seemed confident and relaxed. All the teachers who knew Jeremy were agreed that he was demonstrating remarkable progress, although his achievement was below that of his peers. With the reporting period at hand, Mr. Broughton wondered, How do I recognize his progress despite his current level of achievement? His colleagues agreed, when asked, that kind words would not undo the damage that would result from giving him a grade of D. What to do? was the question in Mr. Broughton's mind.

. . . .

*T*he first nine chapters of this book are organized according to the sequence inherent in the model of assessment and evaluation presented in Chapter Three. There are, however, important general issues relevant to assessment and evaluation that fall outside this sequence. These will be considered here.

Different Demands on Administrators and Teachers

In many cases, where the term *evaluation* is applied to a particular set of actions in a specific setting, the word is unambiguous. However, when different members of the educational community are discussing the issue of evaluation, there is frequently an unexamined assumption that everyone is talking about the same thing, and such is not the case. Administrators and teachers evaluate different things for different purposes, and thus they need different means of assessment and different forms for reporting their findings. An unexamined gap in perceptions can lead to misunderstanding, poor decision making, and considerable unnecessary human suffering. All sections of the educational community ask legitimate but different questions. Misunderstandings arise when the concerns and requirements of one part of the community are imposed on another. No one has a privileged position, and no one holds a monopoly on validity or reliability.

> Administrators and teachers have valid but differing viewpoints.

Administrators and teachers differ in the purposes they have for evaluation, the audience for which the evaluative data is intended, the form of their reports, the contextual nature of data-gathering procedures, and the psychological distance between evaluator and those evaluated.

Purposes

> Administrative decisions result in long-term change.

Administrators are called upon to formulate, implement, and guide broad policy. They make far-reaching decisions. With regard to language instruction, administrators need to know in general terms whether present programs are working satisfactorily. If not, they must ask what changes should be made. Should we buy a new basal reading program? If so, which one? Or should we move to a literature-based program? These are legitimate questions that administrators ask. Although the decisions themselves are relatively simple, the consequences impinge on thousands of individuals for long periods of time. Children, teachers, and parents have to live with administrative decisions that may extend over five, ten, or fifteen years. The learning experiences of whole generations of students may be affected by a single administrative decision.

Teachers, on the other hand, are concerned with the ongoing instruction of individuals. They look at past and present performance in order to predict a child's educational future. These are some of the questions teachers ask: Should I reteach this unit next year? Should I increase the amount of direct instruction? Should Jean work with another child? Does Jeremy need special assistance? Does Joan need to be relieved of some of the pressure she is under?

Audience

Administrators gather evaluative data for themselves, for representatives of the public who sit on school boards, and for the public at large and parents as a group. These audiences need a picture drawn in broad strokes. Evaluative data is used to assure taxpayers that public money is being spent responsibly or that problems in the system indicate the need for a reallocation of resources.

Teachers, on the other hand, gather data for themselves, for the children, and for individual parents. When teachers report assessment and evaluative judgments, generally they do so not to parents as a group but to the parents of Jean, John, Joan, and Jeremy, for example. Their audience is intensely interested in the fine detail of individual performance.

Teachers are involved with individuals.

Form of the Report

Administrators need to know the overall performance of large numbers of individuals. A superintendent who wishes to know if a newly implemented program is working cannot read anecdotal comments for each of the several thousand children in the system. A global summation of the overall performance of the group is needed. Such information is usually expressed numerically.

Teachers need to report the strengths and weaknesses of individuals as each child attempts to cope with a specific curriculum and a finite set of instructional activities in order to acquire complex abilities such as reading, writing, speaking, and listening. It is not possible to summarize the overall performance of a human being in a number or a letter grade. In order to describe the individual's language capacity, the teacher needs

System analysis is reported numerically.

Letter grades do not capture the complexities of achievement.

to use the power, range, and subtlety that a full command of language permits. The dignity due to every individual demands description in a comprehensive statement that provides as full and rounded a picture as possible.

Context

The responsibilities of administrators go beyond the local concerns of individual teachers and classrooms. While giving full recognition to the right each teacher has to teach in ways she or he finds effective, the administrator needs to know if the overall program is working adequately. Assessment devices to answer such broad concerns cannot be based on the specific practices of an individual teacher. Administrators are obliged by circumstance to use decontextualized measures such as standardized tests. The same assessment devices must be applied to all if reliable comparisons of performance are to be made. Such measures must be based on broad aims or generally desired outcomes rather than on the specifics of any particular classroom.

Standardized measures do not usually relate to specific curricula.

Evaluation by teachers is centered in the classroom context. The teacher reports on how the student functions with a specific curriculum, and this is expressed through particular methods and finite materials. The teacher can take into consideration such local concerns as teacher-student relationships, peer influence, and home background. No teacher should label a child as a number or a letter grade, but rather should see individuals as complex human beings functioning in a complex social situation.

Psychological Distance

Administrators usually do not know the children they evaluate. The superintendent does not see the anxiety written across a student's face or feel the clamminess of a student's hands as a test paper is being distributed. In this sense, then, administrators work by proxy. They do not normally administer the tests that will generate the data upon which they will make their decisions.

Students react in different ways to tests.

On the other hand, teaching is a very personal activity. Effective teachers come to know their students intimately. Most of the time, teachers develop a close, warm relationship with each student. Group-administered tests that require teachers to follow written directions ask them to adopt a discordant role. The wise counselor is suddenly suspended on the day of the test, replaced by a test administrator.

Teachers evaluate most effectively as they observe their students dealing with curriculum content, watch the processes children go through when they attempt to solve problems, and offer assistance in carefully judged amounts to determine just how much help particular children need with specific problems.

Evaluation means different things to teachers and administrators. However, both groups have equally legitimate concerns. Both have valid reasons for the questions they ask and the kinds of answers that they require.

Both administrators and teachers have legitimate concerns.

Numerical Data

Real disservice occurs when test information is used to undermine teachers' confidence in their own judgments. There are cases where children, whose classroom performance had been judged satisfactory by their teachers, were placed in special remedial programs on the basis of a single test score. Enrollment in enrichment programs is sometimes determined by a single score on a group-administered standardized test. Such cases are gross examples of test procedures that produce useful information for one segment of the educational community but are misapplied to another. This results in damaging decisions.

Both administrators and teachers need to respect each other's rights and concerns. Teachers need to recognize that while the collection of standardized test data may seem to be a disruption in the classroom, it can produce information suitable for monitoring the overall performance of the system. Administrators need to recognize that the kind of data they value is not of much use to teachers in dealing with individuals. Nor are detailed descriptions of individual performance useful to administrators in assessing the overall effectiveness of a program.

The concerns of all stakeholders need to be acknowledged.

The Myth of Normal Distribution in Education

Modern Western societies endorse the idea of universal literacy. It is assumed that everyone can learn to read and write. However, this notion is in conflict with the assumption that reading and writing abilities are normally distributed. It would be equally possible to devise a walking test, which would show that the ability to walk (or sit or stand) is normally distributed. But why would anyone want one? Society does not hold superwalkers in high public esteem. They are not paid high

Education should not result in normally distributed achievement.

salaries or held up as models for the young to imitate. Nor is there particular concern with the C− walkers. As long as individuals can stumble to work each morning, any relative incapacity is overlooked. The only concern expressed is for those people whose capacity to walk is so limited that it interferes with their ability to meet their daily tasks and aspirations. For these, therapy or prosthetics in the form of braces, crutches, or wheelchairs are provided.

Reading and writing are much like walking, sitting, or standing in that society's concern is to ensure that everyone can achieve a level that is sufficient to arrive at normal expectations. Society does not want reading and writing to be normally distributed. The goal is for everyone to be able to achieve functional competence. Technically, the distribution of literacy should be skewed to the right (Figure 10–1). Normal distributions are assumed to result from random factors. However, education should be anything but random. Therefore, its outcomes should not be normally distributed. Clear educational goals are specified: teachers implement programs to attain those goals and apply differential support depending on the results. Where a child is self-directive, further exploration is encouraged; where a child is hesitant or confused, extra help is offered. Such a differential response in one particular direction should produce a distribution skewed toward the educational goals. In an ideal world with a perfect education system, the distribution would look like Figure 10–2.

In this ideal world, everyone achieves minimal competence; a few are comfortably competent, and some are highly competent. In a real world run by faulted human beings, however, a more reasonable expectation is a distribution such as that shown in Figure 10–3. In this case, there are a few individuals for whom the system has not worked. Functional competence must be continually redefined. In a 19th century agrarian society, functional literacy was one thing. In a late-20th century technological society, functional literacy is something quite different. A normal distribution is undesirable and educationally unsupportable.

Education is not random.

Functional competence changes as society evolves.

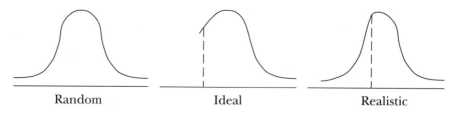

Random   Ideal   Realistic

Figure 10–1 **Three Distributions**

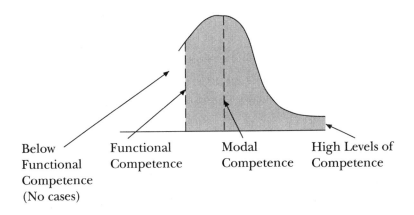

Below   Functional   Modal   High Levels of
Functional   Competence   Competence   Competence
Competence
(No cases)

Figure 10-2 **An Ideal Distribution**

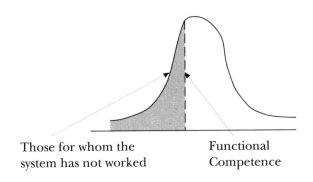

Those for whom the   Functional
system has not worked   Competence

Figure 10-3 **A Realistic Distribution**

Any test that produces a normal distribution of reading or writing behavior is presenting a distorted picture. Test makers have let their assumptions regarding the nature of a chance-based, normative distribution lead them to a selection of test items that produce such a distribution. The discriminatory power of such tests is based on a sample of abilities that is not reflective of the abilities actually used by readers and writers in the real world. Standardized reading tests overemphasize vocabulary and sentence length. These are important features in determining textual complexity, but they are not the only important features. The reader's capacity to deal with cohesion, coherence, text structure, and the application of relevant world knowledge are also important, but these are rarely tested.

Coming to Terms with Standardized Tests

In Chapter Two, some myths and misconceptions about assessment and evaluation were reviewed. It was suggested that norm-referenced, group-administered standardized tests were inappropriate for individual student assessment. For this reason, standardized tests were not included in the data-gathering Quad, nor has their use been advocated as a means of gathering data in assessing individual achievement.

Nonetheless, many teachers are obliged to administer standardized tests in their classrooms. Neill and Medina (1989) have estimated that over 105 million standardized tests are administered to 39.8 million students each year in the United States. Despite the well-documented misgivings (Hoopfer and Hunsberger 1986; Cohen 1988; Haney and Madaus 1989; and Pikulski 1990) there is no evidence to suggest that the use of these tests is likely to diminish. The role of standardized tests for classroom assessment remains a divisive issue for teachers.

. . . .

Standardized tests continue to be widely used and misused.

It is critically important that all stakeholders be aware of the most common misunderstandings about standardized tests in order to guard against their misinterpretation and misuse. Cohen (1988) summarized his concern in this way:

> There are only two things wrong with commercially published NRST's (norm referenced standardized tests) of achievement, aptitude and intelligence—they don't measure what we teach and even the best of them are an inaccurate measure of individual scores.

This warning is so familiar that many educators are lulled into believing that flagrant misuse of standardized tests no longer occurs. Surely in this day and age, no one would persist in practices that have been so resoundingly discredited. Yet there is continuing evidence that the call for vigilance and awareness of abuses needs to be reiterated. Concerned with accountability, many administrators and teachers accept standardized tests because of pressure from the public and from historical convention. For some, this leads to looking for a standardized test that "gives all the answers," as was advertised in one recent professional journal.

This is precisely why teachers need to be knowledgeable about the interpretation and use of such measures. From the perspective of a class-room teacher, there are two features of standardized test scores that need to be critically examined: the meaning of grade equivalent scores and the standard error of measurement.

Grade Equivalent Scores

As was previously noted in Chapter Two, there is a common misunderstanding of what grade equivalent scores (GES) represent. Consider the example of a fourth-grade student who achieved a raw score of 76 on a standardized test that was administered in the eighth month of the school year. When the conversion tables included in the testing manual were consulted, this raw score was found to convert into a GES of 4.5—that is, grade four in the fifth month. The question remains just how to interpret a GES of 4.5 for this student. Does this score signal that there is need for concern about the achievement of the child?

In order to begin to answer this question, we illustrate the way in which grade equivalent scores are determined, using the elementary version of a mythical True Reading Inventory for Children (TRIC-E). The test developers wanted to include a table of grade equivalent scores in the TRIC-E test manual. First, they selected a representative number of elementary classrooms and had all the children write the test in October. As would be expected, a wide variety of scores was reported for each classroom. Nonetheless, when all the scores for all the fourth-grade students were averaged, the mean raw score for grade four in the second month (4.2) was found to be 67.9. The average raw score for all the fifth grade students was 92.2. Of course, no student actually scored 67.9 or 92.2 because on individual tests only whole number results were possible.

These two averages were then used as reference points, and the intervening scores were projected, a process called interpolation (see Figure 10-4, p. 132). As a result of the interpolated scores, a chart of hypothesized raw score conversions was developed. The grade equivalent range that is reported on the conversion chart is not the true range found when the testing was done. Rather, it is simple arithmetic distribution of scores between two known averages. The true range of scores for students at 4.2 was much greater than 67–69. In fact, it would be peculiar if all the fourth-grade students who were tested scored only 67, 68, or 69. The point to remember is that the numerical value of a grade equivalent score does not represent an expected performance level for students at a par-

Grade Equivalent:

4.2	4.3	4.4	4.5	4.6	4.7	4.8	4.9	5.1	5.2

Average Raw Score:

67.9	70.6	73.3	76.0	78.7	81.4	84.1	86.8	89.5	92.2

Grade Equivalent Range:

6.9	7.2	7.5	7.7	8.0	8.3	8.5	8.8	9.1	9.4
6.7	7.0	7.3	7.6	7.8	8.1	8.4	8.6	8.9	9.2

Figure 10–4 **Interpolation**

ticular time in a particular year. It is exactly this common misconception that has cast the use of Grade Equivalent Scores into disrepute.

Standard Error of Measurement

The standard error of measurement should be recorded with a standardized test score.

A second area for concern in standardized tests is the credibility of the numbers themselves. Whenever someone takes a test, there are variations in scores that result from a variety of factors like test-taking experience, time of day, anxiety, and even the weather. The producers of standardized tests are aware of these chance variations in scores and usually report them in the testing manuals as the *standard error of measurement* (SEM). The SEM for the Reading Comprehension subtest of the Stanford Diagnostic Reading Test, for example, is 2.7. Suppose that a student received a raw score of 53 on this subtest. That would convert to a grade equivalent score of 4.7. However, the standard error of measurement of 2.7 means that the "true" score has a high probability of falling somewhere between 55.7 (53 + 2.7) and 50.3 (53 − 2.7). In terms of grade equivalence, then, the student's "true" score is in the range of 4.2 and 5.3. All that can be said with certainty about a student who receives a score of 53 is that the performance is approximately that of students who were in the fourth and fifth grades in the norming sample.

Measurement of achievement is not as precise as numerical scores suggest.

It should be clear from these two examples that standardized measures are not the precise indicators of performance that their numerical character suggests. We agree with Pikulski (1990) that the misuse and misinterpretation of standardized tests must be curtailed, that they need to be placed in context with other information, and that efforts should be directed toward improving them.

In those jurisdictions where standardized tests continue to be mandated in assessing individual performance, there are a number of things teachers can do to deal with this dilemma.

RAISE THE ISSUE: If tests must be given and test results reported, then contractual obligations must be fulfilled. However, professional views should be communicated to colleagues and administrators. Educational decisions based solely on a test score cannot be supported.

PREPARE CHILDREN FOR THE TEST: If tests are required, it is in the best long-term interests of the children that the scores reflect as faithfully as possible the gains that the children have made. Children who are accustomed to sharing their interpretations of meaningful texts may be confused by test items that ask them to respond to nonmeaningful aspects of texts, decontextualized words, and a series of very brief, unrelated passages followed by multiple-choice questions. If standardized test scores are to be reflective of ability, children need to be familiarized with the format and the problem-solving strategies demanded by these tests.

> **Children must be prepared to handle test formats.**

Coaching for a test is far from an optimal educational practice. Nevertheless, the practice remains necessary as long as teachers, programs, and children are evaluated by test scores. Coaching should take place on items that parallel those used in the test. Rehearsal of actual test items is illegal and produces meaninglessly inflated scores that are readily detectable when contrasted with scores from comparable populations.

Therefore, coaching should involve only general test-taking strategies such as:

> Read all directions carefully. Highlight key words in the directions. When completing comprehension items, read the questions before reading the passage.
>
> In selecting among alternative answers, eliminate unlikely possibilities and, if necessary, guess. Don't leave any question unanswered.
>
> Do all the items you find easy first. Then go back to the more difficult problems. This is particularly important when a test is timed.

In addition to such strategies, children should be taken through an analysis of each type of question they will encounter on the test. The teacher should be sure that the children clearly understand what is required of them. Some examples follow:

Sample Test Item 1

Teacher's Commentary

The exercise has three parts: the directions, a passage, and two problems. Read each part carefully.

Read the sentences. Mark the bubble beside each answer you think is correct.

DIRECTIONS. The directions tell you what to do. As you read them, notice beside each answer the key words. Underline them.

mark   The word *mark* means fill in, shade, or color in.

bubble   The bubble is the small circle beside each answer.

correct Only one of the four answers is correct. The other three are wrong. You are to find the one that is correct. *Correct* means that the answer agrees with what it says in the passage.

Janice dressed quickly and hurried into the kitchen. Father was fixing breakfast.

THE PASSAGE. As you read the passage, try to imagine what is happening. Try to make a picture in your mind. Think of someone quickly putting on clothes. Try to see Janice hurrying into the kitchen. Imagine Janice's father getting the breakfast ready. What might he be doing?

1. Find the word that means the same as *quickly*.
   ○ slowly
   ○ fast
   ○ hot
   ○ warm

THE PROBLEMS. Each problem has a direction. Deal with them one at a time.

IDENTIFYING THE PROBLEM. Notice the keywords.

find   *Find* means choosing from the four answers listed below the direction.

means the   This phrase means that you are to look
same as   for the word that could be used instead of the word *quickly* without changing the meaning of the sentence in the passage.

SOLVING THE PROBLEM. Find the word *quickly* in the passage. It is used to tell you how Janice got dressed. The sentence also tells you Janice *hurried*. You should have a picture in your mind of Janice getting ready in as short a time as possible.

Look at each answer in turn. Each time, decide if it could be used instead of the word *quickly* in the first sentence of the passage.

slowly   The word *slowly* ends the same way as *quickly*, but it does not mean the same thing. *Slowly* means the opposite of *quickly*. Do NOT mark, shade, or fill in the bubble beside the word *slowly*.

fast   The word *fast* could be used instead of *quickly.* "Janice got dressed *fast.*" The word *fast* means the same thing as *quickly.* Fast is probably the correct answer. To be sure that *fast* is the correct answer, check the other two words on the list.

hot   The word *hot* has nothing to do with getting dressed. "Janice got dressed hot" sounds silly. Do *not* fill in the bubble beside *hot.*

warm   The word *warm* cannot be used instead of *quickly.* It does not have the same meaning as *quickly.* Leave the bubble beside warm *unmarked.*

It looks as though *fast* is the best answer. Fill in the bubble beside the word *fast.*

REFLECTING ON THE SOLUTION. To get this problem right, you had to use information from four places.

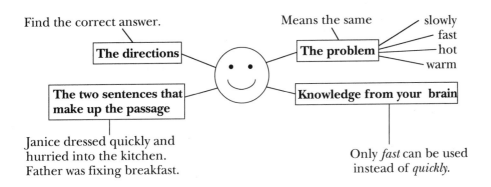

Find the correct answer.

The directions

The two sentences that make up the passage

Janice dressed quickly and hurried into the kitchen. Father was fixing breakfast.

Means the same

The problem

slowly
fast
hot
warm

Knowledge from your brain

Only *fast* can be used instead of *quickly.*

Sample Test Item 2

Janice got dressed quickly and hurried into the kitchen. Father was fixing breakfast.

2. Who was cooking breakfast?
   O Janice
   O Father
   O Mother
   O The maid

Teacher's Commentary

IDENTIFYING THE PROBLEM. The second problem asks, "Who was cooking breakfast?" In this problem, you must choose the answer that correctly answers this question.

SOLVING THE PROBLEM. Only one of the four choices is correct. Look at each choice in turn.

Janice	Neither sentence says anything about Janice doing anything with breakfast.
Mother	There is no mention of Mother in either sentence.
Father	The second sentence says Father was *fixing* breakfast.
The maid	There is nothing said about a maid in either sentence.

Father looks like the best answer. When used in the phrase *fixing breakfast,* the word *fixing* means the same as *cooking. Fixing breakfast* and *cooking breakfast* mean just about the same thing. The second sentence tells you that *Father* was fixing breakfast, so *Father* is the best answer. Fill in the bubble beside the word *Father.*

REFLECTING ON THE SOLUTION. In solving this problem you need to use information from four places.

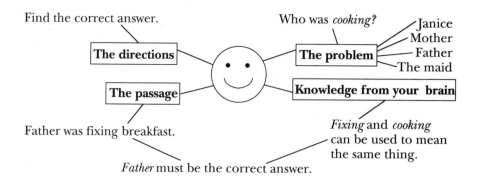

Such detailed modeling need not be prolonged. However, it should be repeated with each type of question. For example, the item below asks the child to address the text at the word-structure level.

> Mark the bubble next to the correct answer.
> The class became very __cited.
>
>   ○ in
>   ○ un
>   ○ ex
>   ○ re

The children need to be aware that they must:

- Read the sentence carefully
- Understand that the sentence tells something about how a class (of children?) becomes
- Provide the sound value of each letter group
- Read the entire sentence each time as they try each letter group in the blank
- Choose the reconstruction that "sounds" right or that seems to make sense

Solving this problem requires the use of four kinds of information.

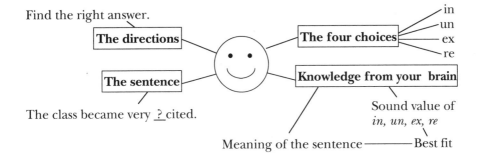

With subsequent examples, the teacher can ask the children what steps they think should be taken and the information they use to find the correct answer.

At a later stage, the children can be given a set of testlike problems to solve. The solutions can be worked on in small groups at first. The children should be encouraged to think out loud. When the problems have been completed, the children can be asked to reflect on their own problem-solving strategies.

Teachers should take care to have the children articulate their thinking processes. "I just knew" or "It just came into my mind" are not reflective responses and should not be accepted. Children who make these responses should be encouraged to say how they knew.

Finally, the teacher should have the children work under conditions like those in the test situation, with individual effort, constrained silence, withdrawal of teacher assistance, time limits, and physical separation of desks.

Children need to learn the test terminology. In some cases, it will require very close examination of test items for teachers to appreciate that certain words are being used in a special way. For example:

top as in "top of the page"	Terms such as *top, bottom,* and *down* presume the print is presented vertically in space. This orientation is maintained even when the text is actually horizontal.
line as in "on the second line."	*Line* is used differently than most children understand. In continuous text, there are no lines drawn on the page.
sound as in "mark the letter that has the same vowel sound as the one in *nice*."	*Sound* is a feature of oral rather than written language. Letters in context may be assigned or associated with sounds when the text is read aloud. Letters themselves are silent visual symbols.
find as in "Find the word that means the same."	*Find* is being used quite differently in this context from the way it is used if someone finds a watch or a silver dollar. *Find* in this context means "From the options listed below, locate and mark one."
bubble	In the child's experience, a bubble is most likely to be a spherical film of soap that drifts in the air with brief and fragile beauty. In the present context *bubble* is a circular, flat, and relatively permanent mark on a page.

The kinds of terms that may need clarification can be found in a publication designed to prepare children for a widely used standardized test. They include words like:

underlined	opposite	almost the same as
compare	facts in the story	phrase
mentioned	blank	makes sense
answer	sentence	directions
questions	problem	paragraph
one that fits best		

However, children do not need coaching on a general list of test-taking terms. They need to be comfortable with the specific terminology used in the test they must take.

It is worthwhile to have the children talk about test-taking and to listen to what they say. Children may be confused, but they are not always aware of their own misunderstandings. One teacher discovered that some of her children, used to responding to texts meaningfully, were very confused because they assumed that the test items formed a meaningful continuity. They believed that the second test item was conceptually related to the first and the third. They were searching for meaning where none existed! It is only through frank and open discussions that teachers have any hope of discovering, and thus correcting, such well-founded confusions. It bears repeating that the coaching practices described here are not the most valuable use of instructional time. Coaching for a test is necessary only as long as teachers and children are evaluated by means of test results.

Letter Grades

In the best of all possible worlds, letter grades would not be used. It is not possible to adequately and justly summarize human performance as a single point along a one-dimensional continuum. All human performance is complex, but language ability is particularly so. It is simply not adequate to say that Alan is a good reader, Beatrice is an average writer, and Candida is a poor speller. Language performance is highly dependent on context. Alan reads science fiction well but is less able to read artistic criticism. Beatrice writes narratives adequately but is a very sensitive poet. Candida correctly spells words to do with dogs (which she loves) but has trouble in other subject areas.

Letter grades do not tell the whole story.

Cindy, a nine-year-old child with Down's syndrome, showed remarkable growth but was not yet performing at a level equal to that of her peers. When she entered her third year of school, Cindy was almost totally lacking in social skills. To obtain the attention she required, she would lie on the floor and scream as she pulled her hair. With patience, modeling, and the care and support of the entire class, Cindy learned how to join a group, how to make appropriate approaches to individuals, how to lace her shoes, and how to use the bathroom independently. She could not read or make any legible marks on paper. What grade is appropriate for Cindy? Should she receive an A for progress or an F for performance? Either grade is distorting and damaging. The A may misinform the parents. The F may destroy Cindy's self-confidence and desolate her parents. The only rational response is to excuse Cindy from the grading process. In narrative form, the teacher can inform the parents of Cindy's progress and indicate the areas in which she might yet develop. No reference to her standing relative to her peers is necessary.

· · · · · · · · · · ·
Anecdotal comments should be informative.

Cindy is used as an extreme case to make a point. The same argument could be applied to many other much less extreme cases, however. In some schools, for example, principals inform certain teachers that they can award no grades higher than C+ because they have the lowest achieving students in their classes.

If letter grades must be used, the criteria for awarding them must be clearly specified. One practice we have found useful involves clearly stating the grades and the corresponding requirements. For example:

C−, C, C+   Fulfillment of all requirements as specified in the assignment(s) and discussed in class.

B−, B, B+   Extension of the assignment (for example, if three pieces of writing are required, the student can submit four or five pieces to earn a B-level grade).

A−, A, A+   Qualitative extension or interpretation of the assignment, which must be made independently by the student. Questions such as, "Would I get an A if . . ." go unanswered.

This procedure works best if pupils submit drafts rather than final copies. The student can then be informed of the grade that the present draft will earn and offered advice on how to raise the grade. Advice on how to earn an A grade is not available, however, because that grade indicates such qualities as initiative, creativity, independence, and/or risk-taking on the part of the student. The student earns the higher grade if all the concerns noted by the teacher on the draft are adequately addressed.

The distinctions between B−, B, and B+ may be left to the discretion of the teacher. Students who feel they have been unjustly graded may present a case. All papers may be revised with a view to earning an improved grade. In this sense, grades remain open to negotiation.

The above procedure tends to redistribute rather than increase the marking load. Marking drafts can become onerous, but the increase in quality of the final product is rewarding. Some absolute increase in workload occurs when students resubmit a revised draft. However, this is exactly where the extra advice has maximum effect. The marking of final drafts is relatively easy, since it amounts to little more than checking to see that concerns raised in earlier drafts have been adequately addressed.

. . . .

Students should be clear about what a grade means.

Marking Children's Written Work

The following procedure for marking children's written work was developed from a suggestion by Williams (1989):

1. If children are writing exploratively, there is no need to formally mark or grade their work. Find something honestly complimentary to say and indicate how the piece might be further developed. Teachers should respond to content rather than concentrate on form.

2. If a formal mark or grade must be given, ensure that all students are doing the same task and that all are aware of the criteria that will be used in judging their work. If students are all working on different tasks, uniform criteria for marking is impossible. One method of proceeding is as follows:

   - Read through all papers quickly without a pencil in your hand. Place each paper into one of three piles: above expectation, at expectation, below expectation.
   - Reread each paper more carefully. Use the negotiated criteria to determine compliments and criticisms to express in marginal notations. Ensure that your critical comments indicate how the paper might be improved.
   - Add a summary comment that is positive in tone. If an inferior grade has been awarded at the intermediate or senior levels, indicate means for improvement rather than just negative criticism. Base your mark or grade on your initial judgment unless it has been modified by a closer inspection of the paper. If a superior grade is given, explain how it was earned.
   - Return the papers to the students and ask them to check your comments and the mark or grade against the negotiated criteria. Make appointments to deal with students' concerns.

A Final Comment on Letter Grades

We believe that teachers should work collectively to negotiate with the administration the right to suspend the awarding of letter grades where appropriate. In recommending the elimination of letter grades, there is no suggestion that judgments about students are not important. It is the thesis of this book, however, that there are much more effective ways than grades to make summative judgments about student achievement.

Chapter 11

Responsive Evaluation: Reporting to Parents

. . . .

Nick tried not looking at them . . . forgetting about them . . . getting on with his project. It didn't work. No matter what he tried to think about, his eyes were drawn back to the pile of ominous brown envelopes, sealed and stacked on the corner of Mr. Ryan's desk. They'd been there all day. Waiting. It wasn't that he was worried, exactly, it was just that . . . well, it would be good to get it over with, that's all.

Three o'clock. Finally, Nick pushed his crayons back in the box, folded his half-colored map, and slipped it into his book. Mr. Ryan tapped his fingers lightly on the envelopes and surveyed the class: "Now, remember, you're to get these report cards safely home to your parents. They'll be expecting them, and in the same condition as I've given them to you. The envelopes are sealed. I know I can trust you all to hand them that way to your parents." One by one, the envelopes were handed out. Nick's was third to the last.

Once clear of the building, the urge to tear the envelope open was strong. Just so he'd know, just so he'd be ready to explain, if explaining was going to be needed. No. It wasn't addressed to him. You didn't open envelopes that weren't addressed to you. He studied his parents' names carefully written across the front. Without really meaning to, he tested the seal with his fingernail. Sealed tight. Holding the envelope against the sun, he strained to detect sense in the faint lines barely visible if he held it at just the right angle. It was no good, he couldn't read it. He'd have to wait. Nick pushed the envelope down into his pocket and pursed his lips. I mean, it wasn't as if he had anything to worry about. . . .

. . . .

*E*valuation should inform. Once information about an individual student has been gathered, sorted, and interpreted, the implications of that information need to be communicated. Communication is a foundational component of a good evaluation model. Traditionally, report cards and reporting conferences have been, and remain, the major means for the sharing of assessment and evaluation information with students and their parents. Unfortunately, traditional report cards and reporting procedures leave a great deal to be desired in this regard.

This section examines some of the critical concerns and decisions that teachers confront when preparing for and presenting reports on their students. The issue of what a report should (and should not) contain is addressed, and specific suggestions for ways of more fully and meaningfully informing both students and parents are outlined. The concept of reporting as a one-way communication from teachers is challenged by the presentation of strategies for transforming the reporting procedure into a genuine exchange of information.

Writing report cards is a difficult and demanding task. The situation described in the following pages is intended to highlight and bring into focus some of the problems, decisions, and questions that arise during the exacting process of translating the enormous array of information available to the teacher into a concise, accurate, and constructive statement about the progress and development of each student.

> **Effective communication is genuine communication.**

> **Report cards take time to prepare.**

Writing the Report

In this section, Josephine is reintroduced. She has just completed the second term of third grade in a primary school. Throughout the term, her teacher gathered, organized, and classified information in an assessment portfolio (Figure 11–1, p. 146). The report cards are due in the principal's office within a week. Josephine's teacher first reviewed the portfolio. What follows is an attempt to reenact the process, which many teachers have frequently experienced.

Mrs. Simmons lifted the slightly bulging and somewhat battered folder out of the box and placed it on the table in front of her. Where to begin? Quickly, she flipped through the contents, thinking of the solemn little girl who sat three desks from the back in the row beside the window. How to make sense of all of this? She glanced through the meager journal entries, then closely examined the anecdotal comments taped to the inside cover of the folder. Funny, she thought she'd managed to record more than just four. Still, she had plenty of writing samples, and she could play the reading tape if necessary. At least Jo tried hard; you had to give her credit for that. Not that it always showed. You only had to look at those scores to recognize that things didn't come easily for her. Mary Simmons picked up the photo of the costume and smiled; she'd almost forgotten about that costume. Jo had positively preened with pride when she'd modeled it for the kindergarten kids. So did her mother, when Josephine told her about it. Well, enough of this or these reports would never get written. Mary Simmons picked up her pen, then tapped it lightly against her palm several times. She flipped slowly through the folder once more. How could anyone be expected to turn all this into a paragraph or two? Josephine's mother never seemed to understand anyway, no matter how clearly the teacher tried to state things. It didn't make it any easier having Harry Underhill always reminding "his teachers" to back up everything with "the facts," either. The facts . . . he almost made it sound as if they made the stuff up. Beginning was the hardest part. Once you had the first sentence—something positive so you started on the right note—the rest usually came more easily. Mary Simmons pushed the folder aside and bent over her paper: "I am very happy with Josephine's progress. . . ." No. "Josephine deserves credit for her positive attitude towards her. . . ." No. After two more false starts, Mary Simmons wrote the following comments about Jo's progress in language arts:

> Josephine is very sociable and friendly. Her outgoing nature allows her to relate well to the other students in her class. Although she has worked steadily through Level B of our reading program, Josephine scored below grade level on the Gates-MacGinitie Reading Test; she ranked 23rd out of our class of 28 students. Her reading, while fluent, lacks expression. She does not always appear to comprehend what she reads and often fails to self-correct mistakes that don't make sense. She operates mostly at the level of literal recall.

Material for the assessment profile must be carefully selected.

Evaluation is data-driven.

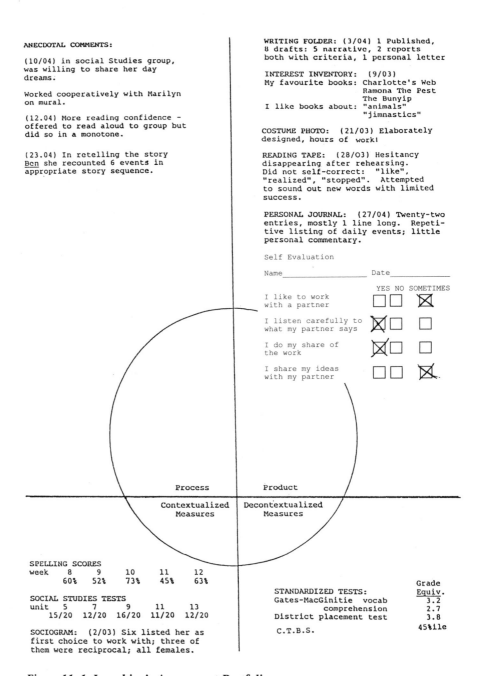

ANECDOTAL COMMENTS:

(10/04) in social Studies group, was willing to share her day dreams.

Worked cooperatively with Marilyn on mural.

(12.04) More reading confidence - offered to read aloud to group but did so in a monotone.

(23.04) In retelling the story Ben she recounted 6 events in appropriate story sequence.

WRITING FOLDER: (3/04) 1 Published, 8 drafts: 5 narrative, 2 reports both with criteria, 1 personal letter

INTEREST INVENTORY: (9/03)
My favourite books: Charlotte's Web
                    Ramona The Pest
                    The Bunyip
I like books about: "animals"
                    "jimnastics"

COSTUME PHOTO: (21/03) Elaborately designed, hours of work!

READING TAPE: (28/03) Hesitancy disappearing after rehearsing. Did not self-correct: "like", "realized", "stopped". Attempted to sound out new words with limited success.

PERSONAL JOURNAL: (27/04) Twenty-two entries, mostly 1 line long. Repetitive listing of daily events; little personal commentary.

Self Evaluation

Name_____ Date_____

	YES	NO	SOMETIMES
I like to work with a partner			X
I listen carefully to what my partner says	X		
I do my share of the work	X		
I share my ideas with my partner			X

Process   Product

Contextualized   Decontextualized
Measures   Measures

SPELLING SCORES
week	8	9	10	11	12
	60%	52%	73%	45%	63%

SOCIAL STUDIES TESTS
unit	5	7	9	11	13
	15/20	12/20	16/20	11/20	12/20

SOCIOGRAM: (2/03) Six listed her as first choice to work with; three of them were reciprocal; all females.

STANDARDIZED TESTS:	Grade Equiv.
Gates-MacGinitie vocab	3.2
comprehension	2.7
District placement test	3.8
C.T.B.S.	45%ile

Figure 11-1 **Josephine's Assessment Portfolio**

When asked to retell or summarize what she has read in social studies or science, she has problems expressing her ideas clearly. She doesn't enjoy reading and has to be prompted to choose books from the library. Those she selects tend to be familiar and easy for her and are almost always fictional. However, when asked to write about her personal experiences she is able to produce properly punctuated, well-constructed sentences. Her contributions to social studies reflect her ethnic heritage. Scores on weekly spelling tests indicate that she has a problem in this area. More practice is required. Additional time spent reading at home, particularly of factual material, also is recommended. Josephine is a nice little girl who adds to our class.

Mary Simmons put down her pen, read over what she'd written, and caught herself thinking "something for everyone." Well, it was true. Facts for Harry, plain English for the Peterouts, with some hints as to how they might help; and some kind words for Jo. Not bad, all things considered. Not bad at all.

The principal, Harry Underhill, read the Peterout report a second time. Mary had warned him that the parents were concerned and that there could be a problem with suggesting that Jo would need to stay a year longer in the primary school. Experience had taught him that it paid to make sure the situation was plainly spelled out on the report card . . . no beating around the bush, no soft-pedalling the truth. It made it a lot kinder in the long run. He could rely on Mary. She didn't mince words, but she said what she had to say nicely, and she was fair. You could tell she cared about her students; just from reading her reports you could see that. Conscientious, too. . . . Nobody would question that Mary had done her homework for these reports. Using red ink, so it would contrast with Mary's black, Harry added: "Josephine is a pleasure to have in our school," and signed his name.

· · · · · · · · · ·

Principals, too, have a voice.

Josephine's report card has been presented at many professional development workshops attended by teachers and principals. Figure 11–2 (pp. 148–49) represents a compilation of the concerns and questions raised during discussions in which participants evaluated this report card in light of the data contained in the assessment portfolio. Teachers were asked to place a check mark beside those comments that appropriately reflected the data and to edit the report so as to eliminate any comments they considered inappropriate, inaccurate, or unsupported by the infor-

Second Report Card
March 5, 1991
Josephine Bilker-Peterout

Josephine is very sociable and friendly. Her outgoing nature allows her to relate well to the other students in her class. Although she has worked steadily through Level B of our reading program, Josephine scored below grade level on the Gates-MacGinitie Reading Test; she ranked 23rd out of our class of 28 students. Her reading, while fluent, lacks expression. She does not always appear to comprehend what she reads and often fails to self-correct mistakes that don't make sense. She operates mostly at the level of literal recall. When asked to retell or summarize what she has read in social studies or science, she has problems expressing her ideas clearly. She doesn't enjoy reading and has to be prompted to choose books from the library. Those she

This is supported by the sociogram and by Josephine's self-evaluation.

This comment repeats what has already been said.

If the standard error of measurement is considered, this judgment might not be accurate with respect to the vocabulary score. Note the discrepancy between the Gates-MacGinitie comprehension score and the score on the District test.

This comment is inappropriate; rankings of this sort should NOT be included in a report card.

This comment is supported by anecdotal data.

The ability to self-correct is highly significant and therefore warrants monitoring. However, the data supporting this claim are limited.

This comment is jargonistic and the meaning may be unclear to parents.

There is no data on summarizing activities in social studies or science. The anecdotal evidence with respect to fiction suggests that summary is not a problem. However, it is not wise to generalize from fiction to nonfiction.

Attitude toward reading is significant information worth noting and reporting. However, no evidence is included in the portfolio to support this judgment, and such a generalization is NOT warranted.
(*continued*)

Figure 11–2 **Concerns and Questions About the Report Card**

selects tend to be familiar and easy for her and are almost always fictional. However, when asked to write about her personal experiences she is able to produce properly punctuated, well constructed sentences. Her contributions to social studies reflect her ethnic heritage. Scores on weekly spelling tests indicate that she has a problem in this area. More practice is required. Additional time spent reading at home, particularly of factual material, is also recommended. Josephine is a nice little girl who adds to our class.

This statement is contradicted by the Interest Inventory; the books listed seem quite age-appropriate and nonfiction is listed as a preference.

No comment is made about the substance or content of her journal entries, only about the form. The journal data indicate a problem of some sort; this is not reported.

This comment is ambiguous and noninformative.

No suggestions are given as to the nature of the practice that should be undertaken. Although seemingly helpful, the comment offers no diagnosis or direction.

This comment is useful and serves to alert parents to how they might be supportive of Josephine.

This comment invariably engenders mixed reactions—it conveys warmth but it is also general and trite.

Figure 11-2 *Continued*

mation provided. They also were asked how they might react to this report card were they one of Josephine's parents.

Questions about the Assessment Portfolio

- Does the information presented represent an appropriate balance of process and product observations, contextualized and decontextualized measures?

- Are enough anecdotal comments provided? Do those that have been gathered offer sufficient support for the comments made on the report?

- Are any of the data contradictory? If so, is there sufficient evidence provided by other sources of information to permit interpretation or resolution of the discrepancies?

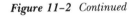

Has the Quad been adequately represented?

The Negotiated Report

If report cards and reporting conferences are to realize the goal of being opportunities for genuine communication, then more than lip service must be paid to the needs and wants of the parents who receive the reports and attend the conferences. Systematic procedures are needed for encouraging and facilitating an interactive exchange of information, and for ensuring that the concerns and questions parents have about their children are addressed in the reporting sessions.

What do parents want to know? What should the model or ideal report card contain? Some time ago, a group of parents who were also teachers attempted to create an example of a "good" report card that could be used as a model. The content of the comment section was debated. Approaching the problem as a parent, each individual had different ideas about what the comments should report. Thinking of what they would want to know about their own children, these teachers placed priorities in different places. The discrepancies were surprising. One called for a comprehensive profile of academic strengths, aptitudes, and interests; another expressed little interest in academics but was far more concerned with social development and peer relationships; one wanted to know about work habits, persistence, and the ability to handle independent and group assignments. While there is no question that all of these perspectives are important, each parent-teacher weighed that importance differently. Clearly, an attempt to devise a model report that would address the information needs and interests of all parents was pure folly, and unwittingly arrogant. Like so many other teachers, this group was ready to decide, *a priori*, what parents needed to know about their children. That different parents want different things is to state the obvious. However, it is a truism that most current reporting procedures do not adequately acknowledge.

As a result of these discussions, a procedure was developed that is now called the negotiated report. It is based on the simple idea that parents need to be consulted prior to the period when reports are written and presented, so that their requests for information can be specifically addressed on the report card and during the parent-teacher conference. The steps involved are outlined below, together with a report of findings from a year-long monitoring of the project's implementation in a large, semirural elementary school.

An exchange of information is part of every parent-teacher-child conference.

What do parents want to know?

Parents should be consulted.

Procedure

1. Involve teachers and administrators in discussions of proposed modifications to the reporting procedure. At an initial meeting, attempt

to clarify goals and strategies, share concerns, and anticipate difficulties. While every effort should be made to encourage all teachers to participate, no one should be forced to do so. Experience has shown that with support from colleagues and the principal, even those initially skeptical are willing to try the procedure. A major goal of this first meeting should be reaching agreement about the nature of an information request form that will be sent home to the parents. At this time, it has also been found helpful to provide models of, and encourage discussion about, the different levels of information that can be provided during the reporting process.

Time constraints do not permit teachers to communicate in depth about a student's progress in every area. Consequently, report cards tend to offer general evaluative summaries on all curricular fronts. These summary statements, which represent a first level of information, usually take the form of grades indicated by letters or other symbols (for example, N = improvement needed), check marks, or brief prose comments. Symbols and marks offer very limited information to parents. All too frequently, written comments also fail to be genuinely informative. Often they do little more than restate the general summary evaluation provided by the letter grade or symbol (for example, "John continues to make good progress in all areas").

A second level of information, called an illustrative anecdote, is therefore recommended. An illustrative anecdote is a summary evaluation with at least one explanatory or illustrative example. For example:

> Chris continues to make progress in reading. This term he has independently selected and completed several challenging novels. During book-sharing sessions, his comments reveal that he reads with insight and enjoyment.

Parents should be invited to identify several areas of special interest or concern. Each area selected by the parent then receives, on the report card, a written illustrative anecdote. The teachers decide the number of areas to be offered for comment.

A third level of information is in-depth analysis. Such an analysis is given orally during a parent-teacher conference. An in-depth analysis includes the following:

- A summary evaluation
- Several illustrative anecdotes, where relevant, from different areas of the curriculum
- An interpretation of the child's growth and development
- Some suggestions for learning strategies designed to initiate, maintain, or improve progress
- A prediction of future progress

Margin notes

Clarify goals and strategies.

Try for consensus.

Evaluation summaries are brief.

Illustrative anecdotes are explanatory.

In-depth analyses are given orally.

The teacher is expected to assemble material relevant to the focus of the analysis (i.e., work samples, projects, interest inventories) to show the parents during the conference. It is certainly not expected that an in-depth analysis be written. The following is an example of the sort of comment that might be made at the conference:

> Jill's reading is progressing satisfactorily. She participates in shared reading and can usually be expected to make a relevant comment about the people or events in the story. She knows to pay attention to the print in order to construct the meaning of the text. She realizes that the text is organized front-to-back, top-to-bottom, left-to-right. She is able to identify only a few individual words, one of which is her own name. She enjoys reading and is happy to try to make sense of familiar texts even though her oral reading isn't always consistent with what is on the page. She deserves praise for her efforts and should be encouraged. Her willingness to try is a very good sign of future progress. In the next few weeks, I anticipate that Jill will identify many more individual words and phrases. From that point on, we may expect to see rapid growth toward independent reading.

2. Introduce negotiated reports to the parents at an informational meeting. This gives them the opportunity to raise questions. Consultation should be genuine; parents' suggestions for modifications or extensions should receive full consideration. The informational meeting can help prevent misunderstandings that might otherwise arise if the request forms are sent home without prior explanation. A full explanation in the school newsletter is recommended for the benefit of parents who do not attend the meeting.

Parents have valid suggestions.

3. Approximately three weeks before the reports are to be written, send parents a letter fully detailing the procedure and requesting that they indicate areas of interest or concern. (See Figure 11–3 for an example of such a letter.) It is important to allow sufficient turn-around time. Parents should be urged to return the forms promptly; a reminder note might be needed.

4. Make note of the parents' requests and take them into account when writing report cards and preparing for conferences. In some cases, teachers will find that they don't immediately have available the information necessary to address a particular parent's request. When this occurs, teachers can attempt to obtain the information in whatever ways are appropriate and practical in the short period of time before the report needs to be written. However, if time constraints render this impossible, teachers should simply inform the parent that they will monitor the situation and

Parents have a right to information about their children.

Dear Parents:

At reporting time, teachers will be reporting on your child's progress during the term. In the past, teachers have reported to you by using the symbols on the report card checklist, by writing comments, and by conferencing with you. Teachers will continue to do this. The change being made this year, is that a month before report cards are sent home and conferences are set, a form will be sent home asking you for your input about what aspects of your child's progress are of the most concern to you. The teachers, with knowledge of your concerns, will then complete the reporting process - responding to your input and adding theirs.

The form sent home will:

1) Remind you that progress in all areas will be evaluated in summary form by using the symbols that are on the report card. The checklist on the report card will be filled in as it has been in the past.

2) Ask you to provide input for the teachers to respond to by choosing up to 2 areas for which you would like an anecdotal comment written on the report card. This provides you with more information about your child's progress than does a letter symbol. In the past teachers have done this, but without input from you.

   The areas will be: Reading   French
                         Writing   Art
                         Listening   Music
                         Speaking   P.E.
                         Mathematics   Social Development
                         Science   Work Habits
                         Social Studies

3) Request you to provide input to help both you and the teacher prepare for the parent/teacher conference by choosing up to 2 areas relevant to your child's development that you would like to discuss during the 15 minute conference with the teacher. You may choose from the list above or add another concern.

The form will be returned to the teachers who can then respond to your input and add theirs.

Sincerely yours,

_____
Principal

Figure 11-3 **Parent Information Letter (Courtesy of Saanichton Elementary School, Saanich, British Columbia)**

will share any findings as soon as they are available. The important thing is for parents to be assured that their request has been noted and that action is underway. The procedure is straightforward, and modifications to regular practice are minor. The effects, however, are not.

Field Testing the Procedure

Negotiated reports were used in a school which has a staff of 20 teachers working with students in kindergarten through seventh grade. The school is located in a rural area near a small city. The parent population, for the most part, is comfortably middle class. The school's experiences were monitored with the procedure over a year-and-a-half period.

Interviews with the teachers, conducted before the parent letters were sent home, revealed several concerns. Almost without exception, the teachers commented on the demands on their time that "normal" report card writing incurred. Estimates ranged from 30 to 90 minutes per report card; most teachers expressed the total time involved in terms of the number of evenings and weekends devoted to the the task. While not begrudging the time, they considered it to be a heavy commitment. Many voiced a concern that the new procedure looked like "more work" and that it would require even more of their time. The space constraints of the standard report card also were suggested as a limiting factor; teachers were concerned that if they reported on all that the parents requested, there would not be room (or energy) left to write comments about those things they felt necessary to cover.

The fear that parents might ask for more information than could readily be delivered led to the teachers' decision to limit to two the number of areas for which parents could request written comments. There was also a measure of unease, especially for teachers of the upper-elementary years, that the parents would request specific comparative information about their children. In other words, most of the teachers were convinced that many of the parents, once given the opportunity, would seek to know precisely where their child stood in comparison to the others in his or her group, class, or grade. Despite these qualms, the teachers appreciated the potential benefits of the consultative procedure and were willing to try it.

Some parents also were interviewed before the modified procedure was announced. The intention was to determine their feelings about the "regular" reporting practices in place in the school. The interviews clearly established that the parents placed far more value on the anecdotal comment sections of the report cards than they did on the marks, grades, and symbols given. Many stated that they found the symbols too general to be

A consultative approach is beneficial.

Anecdotal comments should inform.

meaningful. This contrasted with a perception of many of the teachers that parents considered the marks and symbols to be the significant part of the report, while the comments were merely pleasant additions. When asked how they would like to see report cards improved, parent after parent called for more room for comments and for comments that offered specific and personalized information. Interestingly, very few parents claimed to want comparative information. What they did say they wanted was an early warning of any problems, and sufficient information to judge whether or not their children were progressing as well as they should be. Although this certainly requires comparison, such comparison is made against a general standard of normative performance, and thus it is not a competitive ranking. The conclusion drawn from these interviews is that the teachers had ideas about the needs and wants of the parents that differed in many significant ways from those expressed by the parents.

Competitive ranking is discouraged.

The information request form that was proposed included risk-taking, self-monitoring, and reflection. However, the teachers felt they needed guidance and practice in observing and collecting this sort of information before they could try to incorporate it into their reports. Consequently, an information request form listing only the standard curriculum subjects was sent home. It cannot be too strongly stressed that teachers must adapt this procedure to their particular teaching situations.

Randomly selected parents were interviewed after the first report, and the entire parent population was surveyed after the second. Parents wholeheartedly endorsed the procedure. Over and over again the phrase "it was really nice to be asked" echoed through the interviews. The following comments are representative of the reactions of many:

- Great idea. . . . The teacher was prepared and could let you know in detail. . . . It helps parents recognize their role. . . . You have a say in what goes on. . . . It's good because the teacher may not even be aware there's a problem.

- It's a good idea—it gave the teacher a chance to really think about what you wanted to know. . . . I got a lot more out of the comments . . . and at the interview I got specific examples. . . . The teacher had it all ready, instead of using up your 15 minutes to hunt up papers . . . that's what happened before.

- The interview went better because of the form. . . . It was more specific . . . more focused. . . . Sure, I'd like to do it again.

- I liked being asked. . . . It let you pinpoint concerns that they might not have noticed.

Some parents noted that they found it helpful having to sit down and decide what they wanted to know about their child. Even parents who felt that the new procedure hadn't actually made much of a difference in their particular cases, because they were actively involved in the school and already enjoyed easy access and communication, endorsed the idea of the negotiated report for "other parents." All wanted the new procedure to remain in place.

The teachers reported a significant increase in requests for the first interview, when compared with previous years. However, the requests for the second interview were fewer than usual. Teachers and parents both comment that the need for a second interview was reduced because of the increased level of information available on the report cards.

The teachers were interviewed face-to-face after each reporting period, and all interviews were tape-recorded. Most of the teachers stated that the modifications had made a difference in their reporting. A considerable number expressed surprise at the nature of the requests made by parents. Where they had predicted a predominance of inquiries about academics, in fact, most of the parents wanted to know about social development, relationships with peers, and work habits. While there was no doubt that almost all of the teachers had initially found the changed procedure more time-consuming, the time burden eased by the second reporting session so that overall, it was no heavier than normal. Parental input was found to have helped focus the writing of the reports, and teachers commented that they felt better prepared for the parent-teacher conferences than they had in previous years. The teachers were heartened by the positive feedback received from the parents, and almost all expressed their willingness to continue to consult the parents about report card content in the future.

During the meetings and interviews with the teachers, several remarked that with the exception of general policy statements, they had received little in the way of specific guidance or direction about how to write report cards prior to the project. Most also felt that their pre-service training had not adequately prepared them in the area of evaluation and reporting to parents. The general consensus seemed to be that while they would have welcomed some assistance, they had been left very much to their own devices to figure out what was expected both with respect to report card writing and reporting conferences.

Although there had been no intention to model the writing of reports, several of the teachers specifically noted that they had used as guides models of the illustrative and in-depth analyses, and that they had found them very helpful. Examination of the reports written during the course of the project clearly showed that many of the teachers had adopted the features of the examples presented at the initial meeting.

The report cards were closely analyzed. A random sample of reports written by each of the teachers during the year prior to implementation and during the implementation year were compared. This proved revealing, and it confirmed the principal's judgment that the general quality of the reports had improved. In comparison with reports written in the year prior to the project, the report cards written after consultation with the parents tended to be longer, more detailed, more specific, and to make greater use of concrete examples. They substantiated the judgments made, offered more comments on the processes and strategies of learning, suggested more often how parents might assist the child, and referred more frequently to parents and teachers working together for the benefit of the child. The following excerpt, taken from the report card of a child in a first-grade class, serves to illustrate many of these qualities:

> J____ has gained confidence in math and can compute the basic facts to ten without the aid of counters. He now must work to gain instant recall of these facts, which will improve his speed. He shows some hesitancy to participate in problem-solving activities or activities that involve new concepts. He still does best when new ideas are retaught to him individually. Direction following is the area that seems to cause J____ the most anxiety. He concentrates very hard on the first part of the directions and sometimes forgets the next part. It helps when J____ is asked to verbalize what he must do prior to beginning the task. I feel confident J____ can overcome this with our support.

Responsive evaluation involves reporting procedures that are more dialogue than monologue. Communication is enhanced. As the field study clearly demonstrates, the effects of using negotiated reports are considerable and positive.

Keeping Parents Informed: Perspectives on Newsletters

As any teacher will confirm, reporting to parents involves far more than an information exchange on report cards and during periodically scheduled parent-teacher conferences. Parents are entitled to clear, accessible information about the goals, philosophy, instructional approaches, and evaluative practices their children will experience at school. Taking this responsibility seriously, many schools and teachers creatively

Anecdotal comments are responsive to student needs.

Responsive evaluation results in informed dialogue.

It is important to keep parents informed.

and effectively employ a variety of media and methods to ensure that parents are kept abreast of changing educational perspectives, curriculum content, special events, and classroom and extracurricular activities. These include orientation meetings, the distribution of information letters and pamphlets, parent libraries, open houses, free access to classrooms, invitations to observe and assist, and the use of home-school liaison personnel. Information distributed by these means provides parents with a frame of reference and the context essential for the accurate interpretation of the comments and evaluations made on formal reports. Without such information, parents are operating in a vacuum, and it is a vacuum that leaves many with little in the way of background other than memories of how things were when they went to school.

Newsletters have long been recognized as one of the most efficient and effective means for establishing and maintaining ongoing communication with parents. In the discussion that follows, we present an example of the sort of newsletter that is particularly valuable because of both the form and the type of information conveyed. Figure 11–4 is a copy of the first page of one five-page newsletter, and Figure 11–5 (p. 160) is an accompanying letter. Both were developed by Diane Cowden and her first-grade students at Cloverdale Elementary School in Victoria, British Columbia. They represent one component of her program for informing and including the parents of the children she teaches (Cowden 1989).

This newsletter was the second in a series of three specifically designed to help parents become more aware of the patterns of development in the acquisition of writing. It was intended to help them better understand the progress their children were making. The newsletter has two noteworthy features. The first is that it is primarily written by the children: each issue contains one "article" from each student in the class, reproduced in the child's own handwriting and with invented spellings left intact. The advantage of this is that parents have available concrete examples of the writing produced by children at differing stages of development, and are thereby familiarized with the range of competence to be expected of children of the age span represented. The articles have been signed, but if the teacher is concerned about the public comparison of achievement, names can be left off. Children are well able to point out their contributions to their parents.

The second feature of note is that the newsletter is accompanied by a commentary from the teacher which directs parents' attention to the indicators of growth displayed by the writing samples in the newsletter. The teacher's comments are specific and informative. Rather than offering only general assurances that the "children are making good progress" and

> **Newsletters serve to inform.**

> **Newsletters can be written by students.**

Figure 11-4 **Grade One Newspaper (Courtesy of Diane Cowden, Hillcrest Elementary School, Victoria, British Columbia)**

April, 1990

Dear Parents,

I hope you will find the samples of the children's written work enjoyable and the accompanying comments informative:

Spelling
- Invented spellings are becoming closer to standard spellings.
- The beginning, ending, and middle sounds are being included.
- The children are willing to tackle any word regardless of its difficulty, thus not hindering their written expression.
- The digraphs (ch, th, sh etc.) are often confused, e.g. "schicn" (chicken).
- They are becoming less dependent on articulation and more on visual memory e.g. "brithday" (birthday), "fo" (of).
- A greater use of short vowels, but far from being consistently correct.
- The concept of the silent "e" with the use of long vowels is not firmly established, e.g. "mad" (made).
- A consistent use of the endings "ing" and "s."
- Sometimes the possessive s is confused with the plurals "s."
- Beginning to use the endings "ar," "er," and "ed."
- Most children know how to spell "they" (tha) and "two" (to), but they are not ready to apply this knowledge to their written work.

Printing
- An improvement in printing skills can be seen with a far greater use of lower case letters and the appropriate use of upper case letters.
- Often the capital "D" will be used to avoid mixing "b" and "d."
- Most children are using spaces between words.
- Fewer reversals are occurring.
- Some children are trying their hand at script!

Punctuation
- Some children are placing periods at the end of the sentence (sometimes only at the end of the paragraph!).
- Some children are beginning to use a hyphen, but not with correct syllabication.

Writing
- The children are now willing to take risks and experiment in their writing. This, combined with the confidence they exhibit about using invented spelling, allows them to express themselves freely in their writing. Their ideas are becoming well developed, and more clearly and fluently expressed. Such comments as "Can we do our journals now?," "We will have to make some signs to go with those pictures," convinces me we have a group of children who will always feel comfortable expressing themselves in writing.

Figure 11-5 **Teacher's Commentary (Courtesy of Diane Cowden, Hillcrest Elementary School, Victoria, British Columbia)**

are "becoming better writers," the parents are provided with precise indicators of how such growth can be determined. Current levels of performance are compared with those evident in earlier newsletters (for example, "Fewer reversals are occurring"). The information is made accessible, but it is not overly simplified or generalized; the concrete examples, along with information presented at parent meetings, make it readily interpretable. The tone is not inadvertently patronizing, and the provision of this information implies that parents are interested and able to act upon it.

Many of the parents who received these particular newsletters and accompanying cover letters were single parents, and others were recent immigrants whose first language was not English. Results from a survey undertaken at the beginning of the school year indicated that the majority felt the best way for young children to learn how to write was by means of copying adult models of correctness and by completing drill and practice exercises. Parents felt strongly that errors and "inventions" should be corrected immediately. Asked to rate the newsletters at the end of the year, these same parents gave them a glowing endorsement and reported finding them extremely helpful. Many claimed that without them, they would not have been able to accept or appreciate the approach to writing endorsed by the school. Comments made in interviews left no doubt that the majority of parents had changed their ideas of how writing is learned, and thus how it should be taught, and had learned a great deal from the examples and insights provided by the newsletters. With regard to reporting, the newsletters gave the parents a frame of reference within which to interpret the teacher's comments and evaluation of their children's progress. The usual 15 minutes allotted to the formally scheduled parent-teacher conferences does not provide sufficient time for general explanations about program content or philosophy. Newsletters and letters, and explanatory inserts attached to the report cards are needed if what is reported is to be maximally meaningful.

· · · · · · · · · ·
**Changes occur in
adult perceptions.**

Student-Led Conferences

Wherever practical, students should be included and actively involved in the process of evaluating their own progress and sharing their perceptions of their progress with their teachers and parents. When students are meaningfully involved in this way, evaluation becomes an integral part of instruction and a learning experience in its own right. A variety of strategies for student self-assessment are outlined in Chapter

· · · · · · · · · ·
**Meaningful
involvement in
evaluation can
instruct.**

Five; the following procedure is designed to give the student a major role in preparing for, and in conducting, reporting conferences. It is based upon the model for student-led teacher-parent conferences developed by Nancy Little and John Allan (1988). These conferences have been successfully implemented in classrooms from grades one to seven. The examples used to illustrate the procedure come from Yvette Gellatly's second-grade class in Richmond, British Columbia, and Andrea Lee's third-grade in West Vancouver, British Columbia.

Many teachers now routinely invite students to accompany their parents to the reporting conferences. In order for the potential of parent-teacher-child conferences to be realized, it is important that the student be given an opportunity to contribute and not simply be relegated to the role of audience-member. With student-led conferences, just as the name implies, the students individually conduct the interview with their parents and are primarily in charge of reporting their progress and displaying and explaining their work. Although they are heavily involved in helping the students plan and prepare for the conferences, during the actual interviews teachers stay very much in the background while the students are "in charge." The goal of such conferences is to provide students with an authentic context for self-evaluation and with an opportunity to assume some of the responsibility for informing their parents about how they are doing in school.

> Students have a unique contribution to make to reporting.

> Traditional roles shift.

Preparing for the Conferences

The first step in planning is to ensure that all involved (parents, students, and teachers) are aware of the rationale for handing over the leadership role to the students. It is also important to stress the goals of increased student accountability, involvement, and control. If the conferences will be undertaken on a school-wide basis, a meeting of the teachers should be scheduled so that any concerns can be discussed. It is important that everyone recognize the educational opportunities for reflection, judgment, decision-making, organization, and genuine communication that the procedure can provide for students. Both parents and students should be informed about the teacher's role in helping prepare for the interviews and in supporting the students throughout the procedure. This can reassure students and avert possible misunderstandings. If the goals and roles are not fully explained, there is a possibility that some parents may at first feel that having students report to parents is an abdication of teacher responsibility. When introducing the new procedure, it is perhaps wise to assure parents that they will still receive teacher-written reports

> The rationale must be clearly explained.

> Teacher and student roles must be clarified.

and that they are welcome to request a "regular" conference with the teacher in addition to the student-led interview, should they wish to do so. It is recommended that student-led conferences be fully explained to parents during an evening meeting, and that a description be included in the school or class newsletter for parents unable to attend. Shortly before the scheduled interviews, an information letter reminding parents of the changed procedure should be sent home (see Figure 11–6).

Well in advance of the conferences, the students should begin to prepare by brainstorming and discussing a list of the sorts of work samples they might wish to share with their parents. These work samples should reflect the full range of subject areas, activities, and projects covered by the curriculum and should be selected so as to provide parents with insight

Success hinges on planning and preparation.

```
Dear Parents,

     Starting this reporting period our class will hold " Student
Led Conferences" in lieu of the traditional parent teacher
format.  You can expect to receive a personal invitation from
your child with the time and dates to share and discuss their
work with them. The goals for the students include:

     - being reponsible for reporting to you how well they are
       doing in school
     - learning to communicate
     - learning to evaluate their work honestly and fairly
     - becoming accountable for work and behaviour
     - learning organizational and leadership skills


     This is an opportunity for you, as a parent, to  display a
positive interest in your child's progress, accept your child's
evaluation of his/her accomplishments and provide your child with
support and encouragement for his/her work at school.

     I will be in the room during the conferences, making myself
available for clarification if necessary.  There will be other
opportunities for you to meet with me if either of us feels that
there is a need.

     Thank you in advance for your interest and cooperation with
this new format.


     Sincerely,

     Yvette Gellatly
```

Figure 11-6 **Parent Information Letter (Courtesy of Yvette Gellatly, James McKinney Elementary School, Richmond, British Columbia)**

into, and information about, what and how their children are learning. Teachers should be available to offer guidance during initial discussions and throughout the period when students select items to show their parents. Each child should be given a file folder or a large envelope in which to store work chosen for presentation during the interview. The folders can be personalized and decorated as the children wish.

During the weeks preceding the conferences, the children should thoughtfully select and prepare samples of their day-to-day work that accurately reflect what they can do and what they are attempting to do. Again, teacher guidance can be helpful at this point. The work chosen should be placed in the prepared folders.

A week or so before the interviews are scheduled, each student should write a letter inviting his or her parents to come to the classroom for the conference and offering several possible days and times for the appointment. Parents are asked to reply, indicating a convenient time. Little and Allan suggest that the students include in the invitations a description of some of the things the parents will be able to see. Students can participate in working out the interview schedule for the class. Conventional parent-teacher interviews generally take about 10 to 15 minutes, and many teachers and parents report finding themselves feeling rushed and frustrated by the limited time available. One of the real advantages of the student-led procedure is that the conferences can be extended without requiring the commitment of additional time on the part of the teacher. Because the students conduct the interviews, more than one can occur at the same time. Consequently, interviews can be allotted 30 or 45 minutes each, and the classroom arranged so that three or four students can meet individually with their parents during the same time period. Although the teacher is always present in the classroom while the interviews are being conducted, and thus available to either parents or students if needed, the task of reporting how each student is progressing is assumed by the student. The more generous time allocation renders the whole process more relaxed and informative and grants parents the opportunity to look through their child's books, to ask questions, and to have them answered.

Preparation involves two important additional steps. First, the students write a second letter to the parents. This letter is placed in the file and produced during the conference. It provides students with an opportunity to point out things that they particularly want noticed and that they feel they do well. The letter also asks the parents to respond with a written comment after they have reviewed the contents of the folder. (See Figure 11–7 for a letter by a girl in third grade, and Figure 11–8, p. 166, for a letter by a boy in second grade.) Writing the letter serves several purposes: it helps the

Students reflect and evaluate as they select work samples.

Students are involved in every aspect of the process.

Time pressures are eased.

Teachers play a pivotal but secondary role.

Students are encouraged to focus on their strengths.

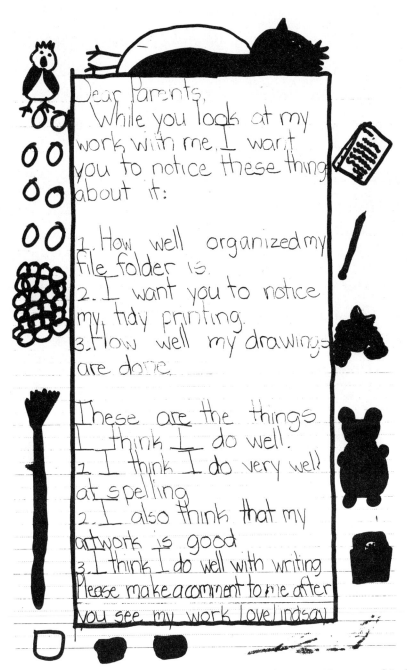

Dear Parents,
    While you look at my work with me, I want you to notice these things about it:

1. How well organized my file folder is.
2. I want you to notice my tidy printing.
3. How well my drawings are done.

These are the things I think I do well.
1 I think I do very well at spelling
2. I also think that my artwork is good
3. I think I do well with writing
Please make a comment to me after you see my work love lindsay

Figure 11–7 **Student-Written Focus Letter for File—Third Year (Courtesy of Andrea Lee, Chartwell Elementary School, West Vancouver, British Columbia)**

Date: _88-11-23_

Dear _Mom and Dad_ ,

While you look at my work with me, I would like you to
notice these things about my work:

how Colorful my pictures are
detail in picters and redding

These are things I do well:

printing, art, running, Krate and
spelling.

These are things I need to improve:

Carpet manners, vice level, Capitals and periods
and printing size.

Please make a positive comment to me:

Curran you always try your best and will do
new things. You seem to be learning well. Remember
to take more time.   — Dad and Mom

Figure 11–8 **Student-Written Focus Letter for File—Second Year (Courtesy of
Yvette Gellatly, James McKinney Elementary School, Richmond, British Columbia)**

children get organized for the conference, it encourages them to review their work and focus on those aspects of it which they consider significant, it provides an opportunity for them to think about their individual strengths and accomplishments. Just as important, this focus letter provides a way for the students to begin the interview: if they initially find themselves at a loss for words, they can start by handing their parents the letter.

Students are supported throughout the procedure.

The final preparatory step required is a rehearsal. Students should practice presenting and explaining the contents of their folders before sharing them with their parents. Buddies from other classrooms make ideal substitute parents. If buddies are not available, then students can take turns presenting their work to a partner. The rehearsal provides a genuine context for each student to receive, in an informal and non-threatening way, reactions and feedback. The student playing the parent role should be encouraged to be constructive and to ask the type of questions parents would likely ask. He or she might suggest, for example, that more background information be provided about particular assignments, that an overlooked item be featured, or that the parents might find it interesting to be shown how a tricky math problem was solved. A positive, interested reaction from the partner can bolster confidence. It is important that this step not be overlooked; experience has proven that it contributes considerably to the comfort of the students and to the smoothness of the interviews.

Practice builds confidence.

When properly prepared, most students have been found (despite some nervousness) to eagerly anticipate the conferences (see Figures 11–9 and 11–10, pp. 168–69). As one boy in his third year of school put it: "I like these cofferences because it is very fun to do. I want my perents to notice my neater printing and my writing and my idea." Another wrote: "Today I'm going to have a coffrence and I aspeshaly want to show my mom my math because I want to show them how well I'm doing, and I also want to show them evry thing. I'm not scaried of showing them anything either."

Evaluation should not be threatening.

Conducting the Conferences

For the interviews, the classroom should be arranged so that there are several distinct areas where the students can talk with their parents with a reasonable degree of privacy. This is easily accomplished by placing tables in different corners of the room. At the scheduled time, each student introduces his or her parent(s) to the teacher, escorts them to one of the tables, and then proceeds to present the work contained in the folder. If time permits, parents also can be shown projects and work displayed throughout the classroom. In Miss Lee's class, some students took advantage of extra time to play new songs on their recorders while others took delight in giving their parents the same tests they had taken.

Students can show what they have learned.

Sonja   9.07.02

Converance

I am excited because I think it's fun showing the things I have done, to my mom or dad. I think my parents like the things we do. But I think it's a little hard to explain the penguin project. What I really want to show my mom is the math book. I can't wate till she rights a coment on my paper.

I love it when our parents make comments about our work as well. yea

my mom

me

Figure 11-9 **Anticipatory Comments—Sonja (Courtesy of Andrea Lee, Chartwell Elementary School, West Vancouver, British Columbia)**

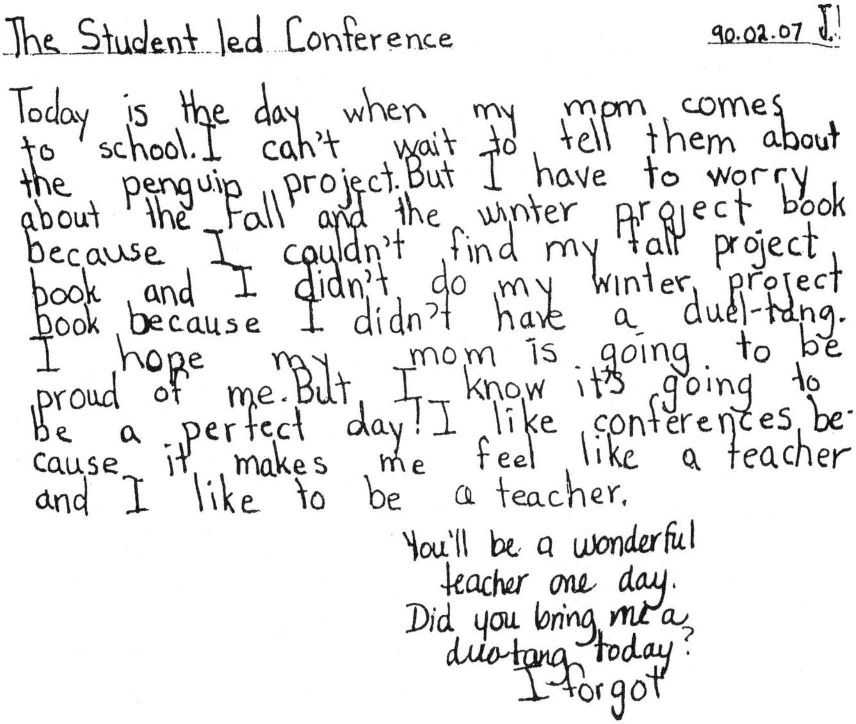

The Student led Conference   90.02.07 J.

Today is the day when my mom comes
to school. I can't wait to tell them about
the penguin project. But I have to worry
about the fall and the winter project book
because I couldn't find my fall project
book and I didn't do my winter project
book because I didn't have a duel-tang.
I hope my mom is going to be
proud of me. But I know it's going to
be a perfect day! I like conferences because it makes me feel like a teacher
and I like to be a teacher.

You'll be a wonderful
teacher one day.
Did you bring me a
duo-tang today?
I forgot

Figure 11–10 **Anticipatory Comments—Jenny (Courtesy of Andrea Lee, Chartwell Elementary School, West Vancouver, British Columbia)**

The teacher is present in the classroom during all of the conferences, and he or she circulates and briefly joins each of the groups as appropriate. The teacher's task is unobtrusively to monitor the interviews to ensure that they are being successfully handled, and to offer support if it is evident support is needed. As far as it is possible, however, the teacher should stay in the background. At this point the role is to give quiet support and encouragement to the students, but to let them direct the interviews. The exception to this would be the case of the over-critical parent. In such an instance, "The teacher intervenes, if necessary, to change the direction of the interview and to strengthen the child's position" (Little and Allan 1988, 19). Similarly, a very shy or insecure child might benefit from having the teacher join the parents at the table for the entire interview.

> The teacher intervenes and assists only when needed.

Once the interview is finished, the child asks the parent(s) to write a comment or two in response to the information presented. This is an opportunity for parents to acknowledge and express their support for, and pride in, their children. Because the comments are written, children can

> Parental comments enhance self-esteem.

read these personal messages from their parents over and over again. While some parents will write only a sentence or two, others will write pages. As the examples presented in Figure 11–11 make clear, parents take seriously this chance to provide praise, encouragement, and advice to their children.

Before the parents leave the classroom, they are invited to sign a classroom guest book. Space should be provided for the date, each parent's signature, and general comments. The guest book provides the teacher with a record of parental attendance and an indication of the parents' reactions to the student-led approach to reporting (see Figure 11–11). As the comments tend to be overwhelmingly positive, the guest book rewards the teacher's efforts with tangible proof that the outcomes have been worthwhile and appreciated (i.e., "This is a terrific classroom—well run and so interesting. Thank you, Mrs. Gellatly, for sharing this time and energy with us."). It can also give the teacher important insights, should parents have concerns. Sometimes the comments point out benefits of the procedure that might not otherwise have been recognized. For example, note the remark in Figure 11–12 (p. 172) that "children need the opportunity to sustain dialogue in such an organized way." Another parent suggested that the conferences provided "good practice for future business presentations."

Once the guest book has been filled in, the student escorts his or her parents into the hall or staffroom, where light refreshments are available. Ideally, these should be prepared and served by the students. This provides an informal, relaxed atmosphere in which all concerned can discuss what has happened.

- - - - - - - - - -
Students evaluate the success of the conferences.

After the Conferences

In the days following the conferences, the students should be given an opportunity to discuss with the teacher and their classmates their reactions and feelings about their interviews. Such a "debriefing" session grants the students the opportunity to reflect on the experience and also to share their perceptions, concerns, and sense of accomplishment. By listening to the students' reactions, the teacher can determine whether the experience was, in fact, a positive and productive one and whether the students required more or different support than that received. In almost all instances, students have reported that they enjoyed the conferences and would like to do them again. Their enthusiastic endorsement of the procedure is clearly evident in the comments written by Miss Lee's third-grade students (see Figure 11–13, p. 173), one of whom proclaimed, "It went really well" three times in the space of one short paragraph.

Feb. 8 '90

Dear Robyn,

Yes you are doing an excellent job in the grade three program. Daddy and I are very proud of your organization, neatness and daily work. I am especially pleased because you do the best you can in everything you do. I think your artwork is very creative with lots of bold colors and attention to detail.

. . . .

Dear Peter,

You conducted the interview in a most professional manner! Your project work is very interesting and I particularly enjoyed your explanation of La Météo. Your math book was particulary neat and well done. I loved your journal. Have you ever thought of checking for spelling? Try to find 3-5 errors every time you write. Your spelling will improve in is time.

Love Mummy

Figure 11-11 Parents' Letters to Their Children (Courtesy of Andrea Lee, Chartwell Elementary School, West Vancouver, British Columbia)

I thought these conferences were very informative & very well worthwhile. Learned a lot. Very well organized & covered a lot of ground in a very short period of time.

This was a great opportunity for the child to explain his work with confidence and in detail. It was a very worthwhile exercise! Children need the opportunity to sustain dialogue in such an organized way.

This Conference is really Good to me to Know about Jenny's Works. I wish Jenny could do more better Work on Maths. Thank You   Miss Lee!

Graham led the conference so well. I'm sure you spent alot of time on it, This made the conference profitable for both Graham and myself.
                                    Thank you.

The conference was a wonderful way for us to share Christina's work. I was impressed with the things she's done, but also her presentation, confidence and pride. I learned alot too. A great opportunity and so well organized. Thank you.

I think the student gains the confidence needed to handle any situation that could be stressful, it gives them the feeling of expressing what they know, and think and the desire to learn, I'm all for it.   more!

This conference is benefitial to both the parents & children in that, the student has a good knowledge of what he learns and what he has achieved.
                        Thank you

Figure 11–12 **Parent Comments from the Guest Book (Courtesy of Andrea Lee, Chartwell Elementary School, West Vancouver, British Columbia)**

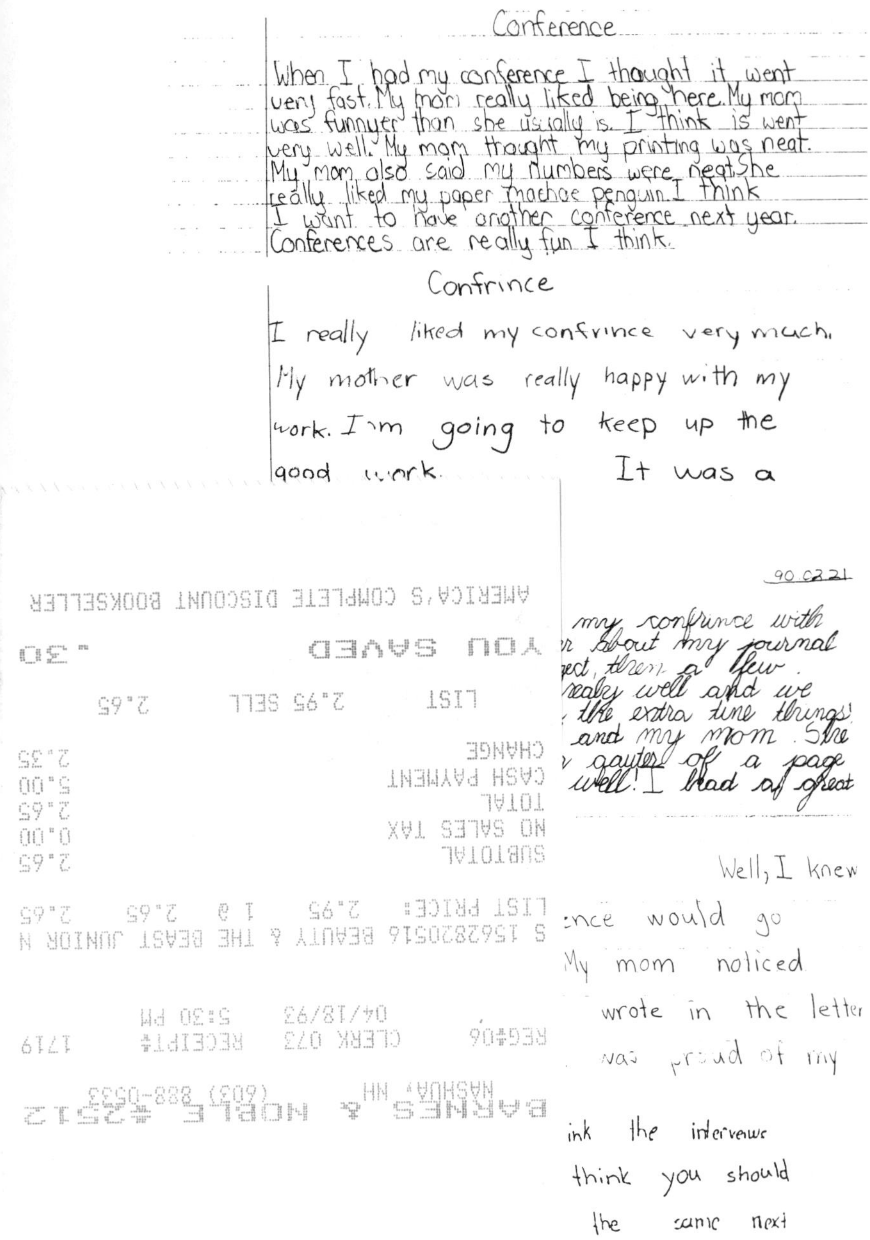

Conference

When I had my conference I thought it went very fast. My mom really liked being here. My mom was funnyer than she usually is. I think is went very well. My mom thought my printing was neat. My mom also said my numbers were neat. She really liked my paper machae penguin. I think I want to have another conference next year. Conferences are really fun I think.

Confrince

I really liked my confrince very much. My mother was really happy with my work. I'm going to keep up the good work.   It was a

90.02.21

my confrince with
about my journal
ect, then a few.
realey well and we
the extra time things
and my mom. She
gaues of a page
well. I had of great

Well, I knew

nce would go

My mom noliced

wrote in the letter

was proud of my

ink the interveiws

think you should

the same next

Figure 11–13 Student Reactions to the Conferences (Courtesy of Andrea Lee, Chartwell Elementary School, West Vancouver, British Columbia)

Clearly, student-led conferences can provide constructive and affirming experiences for the students. As the comments in the guest books have confirmed, parents also find the interviews rewarding and informative. One of the positive side benefits has been increased parental attendance at the reporting conferences. Many of the teachers we work with have found that all parents attend. It is worth noting that although parents are told they may request an additional "regular" interview with the teacher, very few choose to do so. Little and Allan (1988) report that an average of only three parents per class ask for teacher conferences. This figure was confirmed in a field study by the authors. When parents do ask for extra interviews, however, it is important that the interviews be scheduled for times different from the student-led conferences, so that students aren't upstaged. Should a parent not be able to come to the school for the child-directed interview, then the folder can be sent home and the student can hold the conference there. Some teachers have arranged a telephone conference, with the child and teacher phoning the parents from the school and then sending the folder home. Minor adjustments can easily make it possible for all to participate successfully.

Student-led conferences exemplify many of the principles that have been advocated throughout this book: Evaluation becomes an integral and constructive part of the learning process. The approach is inclusive and consultative, and it grants the student an active and meaningful role in assessing and interpreting his or her learning. Accountability and responsibility are built into the self-assessment process; self-respect and self-esteem are enhanced; the students are asked to focus on strengths and to give their own perspective on areas they are trying to improve. The teacher plays a key role, but it is one very different from that normally played in reporting conferences. The teacher structures the situation; offers ongoing, positive, and practical support; and makes it possible for the student to move into a leadership role.

· · · · · · · · · · ·

Parents find the conferences genuinely informative.

· · · · · · · · · ·

Absent parents can be accommodated.

· · · · · · · · · ·

Accountability is personalized.

· · · · · · · · · ·

Evaluation enhances learning.

Chapter *12*

An Action Plan

Frank closed his book on evaluation, put it down, and stared into space. His thoughts came quickly: "As principal of this school, clearly I need to generate some changes. But how will my staff respond? Will they be willing to get involved in a totally different assessment and evaluation program—even if they are convinced it is worthwhile? And what about the parents? What will they think?" More thoughts surfaced for Frank. "I know we have a wonderful program. It's research-based, and everyone is really growing—pupils and staff. But our methods of assessment and evaluation haven't changed for ten years: not since I've been here, in fact." He glanced at his bulletin board and noticed that his secretary had pinned up a new slogan: "Don't try. Begin one step at a time and just do it." He smiled. "Hmmm. . . ."

*T*his book, in itself, is an action plan for change in assessment and evaluation as currently carried out in our schools. The major focus of the book has been to provide a perspective for change in the way in which we assess and evaluate literacy. There are principles of literacy assessment and evaluation that should not be violated, and there are many current myths and misconceptions that must be addressed. A model of assessment and evaluation has been developed, and a data-gathering profile suggested. It has been stressed throughout that parents should be consulted and included both in the education of their children and in the literacy assessment and evaluation programs practiced in our schools. Means of data collection and the interpretation of information gathered have been discussed, and assessment and evaluation in an integrated classroom highlighted. The necessity for being responsive to parents concerns was signaled. Finally, troublesome issues that won't go away have been discussed.

As teachers and administrators are faced with changing curricula, public demands for excellence, and an increased focus on accountability, what is known must be translated into what is implemented in the classroom. Specifically, then, what can be done?

In the short term, teachers and administrators must become knowledgeable about assessment and evaluation issues and about the appropriate practices that follow from these. How? They can form support groups where topics of concern are researched and discussed. These can be constituted within a school or across a number of schools: what is important is to rationalize the relationships between aims or goals, curricular implementation, and assessment and evaluation. Teachers and administrators can also encourage and plan in-service sessions focused on topics of concern. They can start a professional library on literacy acquisition and on assessment and evaluation.

Also, in the immediacy of classrooms and schools, teachers and administrators can begin to modify their practices by enriching approaches to assessment and evaluation. One of the first steps is to implement profile assessment and organize classrooms so that this does not become a burdensome and overwhelming task.

Daily activities and their resultant products can become the basis of assessment profiles. Rather than think of teaching and evaluation as separate processes, teachers can integrate them into a unified whole simply by the perspective they adopt. What is needed is a shift in our awareness of the importance of ongoing, daily activities. These are not secondary

Everyone needs an action plan.

Knowledge is important.

Begin to modify current practices.

Teaching and evaluation are integrated.

to assessment and evaluation but rather, in the main, are the "stuff" of which assessment and evaluation are made.

It is relatively easy to include parents in assessment and evaluation activities, and this signals a shift in responsibility for literacy assessment and evaluation. As educators become more knowledgeable, it is important for them to inform parents about changes they are making both in the classroom and in assessment and evaluation procedures. Clarifying programs, and establishing real communication links with parents, is an appropriate beginning. As educators invite parent involvement, they come to realize that parents have much to offer them. Teachers can begin to develop worthwhile reporting relationships with parents by including them and their children in discussions about current progress and future directions that might be taken.

Parents are involved.

Many teachers feel powerless in the face of administrative or jurisdictional mandates that include, for example, standardized tests. However, such mandates in no way prevent teachers from developing worthwhile assessment and evaluation programs. If assessment techniques external to the classroom must be used, they simply provide one more piece of information for purposes of evaluation.

Standardized tests do not preclude developing a worthwhile assessment and evaluation program.

In the long term, changes in assessment and evaluation policies and practices will occur only as a result of a better-educated populace. Educators have an important part to play in this. They can consult and negotiate with professionals at every educational level. They can ensure that jurisdictional priorities are set in the light of current theory, local needs, and the present level of awareness of their constituents. They can establish clarity, consistency, and coherence in their systems and can work for change in schools, districts, and provinces or states. They can serve on school, district, and provincial or state committees and can take responsibility for providing appropriate alternatives for present local practices. Finally, they can get involved as active participants in their own learning and as responsible professionals in the decisions that are made in schools. Every individual can make a difference in developing and implementing a perspective for change in literacy assessment and evaluation in schools. Such is the mark of a professional educator.

Educators should lead the way.

Everyone should become involved.

References

Anastasi, A. 1967. Psychology, psychologists and psychological testing. *American Psychologist* 22: 297–306.

Atwell, N., ed. 1990. *Coming to know: Writing to learn in the intermediate grades.* Portsmouth, N.H.: Heinemann.

Bloom, B., M. Engelhart, E. Furst, W. Hill, and D. Krathwohl. 1956. *The taxonomy of educational objectives: The cognitive domain.* London: Longman.

British Columbia Ministry of Education. 1988. *A legacy for learners: Royal Commission report on education.* Victoria, B.C.: British Columbia Ministry of Education.

———. 1989a. *British Columbia Draft Curriculum Revision.* Victoria, B.C.: British Columbia Ministry of Education.

———. 1989b. Oral Language Resource Guide. Victoria, B.C.: Evaluation Branch.

———. 1989c. Language Arts English: Grades 1–12, curriculum guide. Victoria, B.C.: British Columbia Ministry of Education.

British Columbia Primary Teachers' Association. 1985. *Evaluation techniques: A handbook for teachers.* Vancouver, B.C.: British Columbia Teachers Federation.

Brown, H. and B. Cambourne. 1987. *Read and retell: A strategy for the whole-language/natural learning classroom.* Portsmouth, N.H.: Heinemann.

Cambourne, B. and J. Turbill. 1987. *Coping with chaos.* Sydney, Australia: Primary English Teachers Association. Distributed in the U.S. by Heinemann, Portsmouth, N.H.

Canadian Council of Teachers of English. 1985. Evaluation policy. *Classmate* 16 (2): 27–30.

Clay, M.M. 1979. *The early detection of reading difficulties.* Portsmouth, N.H.: Heinemann.

Cleary, B. 1968. *Ramona the pest.* New York: Dell.

———. 1977. *Ramona and her father.* New York: Morrow.

Cohen, A.S. 1988. *Tests: Marked for life.* Toronto: Scholastic.

Cowden, D. 1989. *Parent, teacher and the emergent writer: A parent participation program.* Master's thesis, University of Victoria, British Columbia.

Davis, J.E. and H.K. Davis, eds. 1988. *Your reading: A booklet for junior high and middle school students.* Urbana, Ill.: National Council of Teachers of English.

Eastman, P.D. 1972. *Are you my mother?* New York: Random House.

Eisner, E.W. 1981. Using professional judgement. *Applied strategies for curriculum evaluation,* ed. R.S. Brandt, 41–47. Alexandria, Virginia: Association for Supervision and Curriculum Development.

Eisner, E. 1983. The kinds of schools we need. *Educational Leadership* 4: 48–85.

Farr, R. and R.F. Carey, 1986. *Reading: What can be measured.* Newark, Delaware: International Reading Association.

Gardener, H. 1983. *Frames of mind: The theory of multiple intelligences.* New York: Basic Books.

Gleick, J. 1987. *Chaos: Making a new science.* New York: Viking Penguin.

Goodlad, J. 1984. *A place called school.* Toronto and New York: McGraw Hill.

Hall, N. 1987. *The emergence of literacy.* Portsmouth, N.H.: Heinemann.

Haney, W. and G. Madaus. 1989. Searching for alternatives to standardized tests: Whys, whats and whithers. *Phi Delta Kappan,* 70:683–687.

Harste, J., V. Woodward, and C. Burke. 1984. *Language stories and literacy lessons.* Portsmouth, N.H.: Heinemann.

Hirsch, E.D. 1987. *Cultural literacy.* New York: Houghton Mifflin.

Hoban, R. 1964. *Bread and jam for Francis.* New York: Scholastic.

Hoopfer, L. and M. Hunsberger. 1986. An ethnomethodological perspective on reading assessment. *Forum in Reading and Language Education,* 1(1): 103–119.

Hymes, D. 1964. The ethnography of communication. *American Anthropologist* 66: 1–34.

Johnson, T.D. and D.R. Louis. 1987. *Literacy through literature.* Portsmouth, N.H.: Heinemann.

———. 1990. *Bringing it all together: A program for literacy.* Portsmouth, N.H.: Heinemann.

Johnston, B. and S. Dowdy. 1988. *Work required: Teaching and assessing in a negotiated curriculum.* Albert Park, Victoria, Australia: Martin Educational, in association with Robert Anderson and Associates.

Little, N. and J. Allan. 1988. *Student-led teacher parent conferences.* Toronto, Ontario: Lugus Publications.

Macrorie, K. 1970. *Uptaught.* Hayden, N.J.: Rochelle Park.

Madaus, G.F. 1989. The influence of testing on the curriculum. *Critical issues in curriculum: Eighty-seventh yearbook of the National Society for the Study of Education,* ed. L.L. Tanner, 83–121. Chicago: University of Chicago Press.

Miles, M. and M. Huberman. 1984. *Qualitative data analysis: A sourcebook of new methods.* London: Sage Publications.

Moffett, J. 1968. *Teaching the universe of discourse.* Portsmouth, N.H.: Boynton/Cook.

Morrow, L.M. 1989. Using story retelling to develop comprehension. *Children's comprehension of text,* ed. K.D. Muth, 37–58. Newark, Delaware: International Reading Association.

Neill, D. and N. Medina. 1989. Standardized testing: Harmful to educational health. *Phi Delta Kappan* 70:688–702.

Newkirk, T. 1989. *More than stories: The range of children's writing.* Portsmouth, N.H.: Heinemann.

O'Dell, S. 1960. *Island of blue dolphins.* New York: Houghton Mifflin.

Olson, A. 1986. A question of readability validity. *Journal of Research and Development in Education* 19 (no. 4): 33–40.

Paterson, K. 1977. *Bridge to Terabithia.* New York: Crowell.

Paulsen, G. 1988. *Hatchet.* New York: Viking Penguin.

Pikulski, J. 1990. The role of tests in a literacy assessment program. *The Reading Teacher.* 43(9):686–688.

Quinn, P.M. 1987. *Creative evaluation.* 2nd ed. Beverly Hills, California: Sage Publications.

Read, C. 1986. *Children's creative spelling.* Boston: Routledge and Kegan Paul.

Rivalland, J. and T.P. Johnson. 1988. Literacy Lifeboat: An environmental approach to writing instruction. *Australian Journal of Reading* 11(1), March: 42–53.

Scrivin, M. 1981. The Radnow evaluation derby. *Applied strategies for curriculum evaluation,* ed. R.S. Brandt, 34–40. Alexandria, Virginia: Association for Supervision and Curriculum Development.

Shapiro, L.L. 1986. *Fiction for youth.* New York: Neal-Schuman.

Smith, F. 1986. *Insult to intelligence: The bureaucratic invasion of our classrooms.* Porthsmouth, N.H.: Heinemann.

Stanovich, K. 1986. Matthew effects in reading: Some consequences of individual differences in the acquisition of literacy. *Reading Research Quarterly* 21:360–406.

Sternberg, R.J. 1988. *The triarchic mind.* New York: Viking.

Sultzby, E. 1985. Children's emergent reading of favorite storybooks: A developmental study. *Reading Research Quarterly* 20: 458–481.

Topping, K. and S. Wolfendon. 1985. *Parental involvement in children's reading.* London: Croom Helm.

Valencia, S. and D.P. Pearson. 1988. New models for reading assessment. *Reading Education.* (Center for the Study of Reading, Champaign-Urbana, Ill.)

Vygotsky, L.S. 1978. *Mind in society: The development of higher psychological processes.* Cambridge, Mass.: Harvard University Press.

Wells, G. 1986. *The meaning makers: Children learning language and using language to learn.* Portsmouth, N.H.: Heinemann.

Wilkinson, A. 1986. *The quality of writing.* Milton Keynes, England: Open University Press.

Williams, J.D. 1989. *Preparing to teach writing.* Belmont, Calif.: Wadsworth.

Woolings, M. 1984. Writing Folders. *English Quarterly* 17 (Fall): 20–25.

Worthen, B. 1981. Journal entries of an eclectic evaluator. In *Applied strategies for curriculum evaluation,* ed. R.S. Brandt, 58–90. Alexandria, Virginia: Association for Supervision and Curriculum Development.

Index

183